REPORT
ON THE
AMARAVATI TOPE

REPORT
ON THE
AMARAVATI TOPE
AND EXCAVATIONS ON ITS SITE IN 1877

BY

ROBERT SEWELL,
OF THE MADRAS CIVIL SERVICE, MEMBER OF THE ROYAL ASIATIC SOCIETY
OF GREAT BRITAIN AND IRELAND, AND OF THE ASIATIC SOCIETY OF BENGAL

PRINTED BY ORDER OF THE SECRETARY OF STATE FOR INDIA IN COUNCIL

GYAN

Published by

GYAN

Gyan Publishing House
5, Ansari Road
Daryaganj, New Delhi-110002
Phone: 011-47034999, 9811692060
E-mail: books@gyanbooks.com

Distribution Network
gyanbooks.com
India, USA, Canada, UK, Australia, France

ISBN : 978-81-212-2115-3 (HB)
First Published, 1880

2nd Impression 2021

Printed at: Gyan Press, Delhi.

Report on the Amaravati Tope
Author: Robert Sewell

REPORT

ON THE

AMARÁVATI TOPE,

AND EXCAVATIONS ON ITS SITE IN 1877.

BY

ROBERT SEWELL,

OF THE MADRAS CIVIL SERVICE, MEMBER OF THE ROYAL ASIATIC SOCIETY OF GREAT BRITAIN AND IRELAND, AND OF THE ASIATIC SOCIETY OF BENGAL.

PRINTED BY ORDER OF THE SECRETARY OF STATE FOR INDIA IN COUNCIL.

LONDON:
PRINTED BY GEORGE EDWARD EYRE AND WILLIAM SPOTTISWOODE,
PRINTERS TO THE QUEEN'S MOST EXCELLENT MAJESTY.
FOR HER MAJESTY'S STATIONERY OFFICE.

1880.

CONTENTS.

ILLUSTRATIONS.

NOTE.

The following Paper is a Report to the Government of Madras under whose orders and by whose sanction the excavations at the Amarávati Tope were conducted in 1877. It is printed by the kind permission of the Secretary of State for India in Council, with the view of obviating the inconvenience and delay which would be caused by submitting it in manuscript.

It is earnestly to be desired that the marbles still in India belonging to this magnificent monument should be transmitted to England. The defaced and damaged specimens now in the British Museum are considered of such value by that great Antiquary and Architect, Mr. James Fergusson, that he has devoted half his splendid work on "Tree and Serpent Worship" to their consideration; but the exquisite specimens still existing in India, are as superior to them as highly polished marble is to very inferior stucco. The stones in India have clear, polished, smooth surfaces, many of them with every line of carving as fresh as when they left the sculptors' hands. Those in England are so defaced as to be almost unrecognisable, while the marble has so deteriorated by careless exposure that it looks like badly whitewashed limestone. If the slabs in England are so valuable, what would not be thought of those now in India? It is impossible to exaggerate the difference in their condition.

It is, however, possible that, at least for the present, no proposal for the transmission of the marbles to this country will meet with approval in consequence of the crowded state of the British Museum, to which Sir Walter Elliot's collection of the Amarávati sculptures has lately been transferred. But at least they could be sent to Madras. At Amarávati the marbles lie buried out of sight, or exposed to the tender mercies of idlers, in an out-of-the-way village seldom visited except by some hard-worked European officer, whose tent is pitched under the trees hard by, perhaps once in six months, and then only for a day or two at a time. 270 miles by road from Madras, and 130 from the nearest railway station, Amarávati is not likely to be a favourite resort for travellers. The Tope is so destroyed that nothing can be gained by leaving the slabs *in situ*, since only a few mutilated fragments remain in their original positions. The marbles should be removed to a place of safety, where, at the pleasure of the scientific world, they could be catalogued and exhibited, or placed exactly as they were found lying when excavated. If left where they are they must be guarded by paid watchmen, at a perpetual charge to the State; for to leave them unguarded, or watched by the hard-worked village officials, is simply to condemn them to mutilation and destruction. The latter proposal can never for a moment be seriously considered. Now there are only two places in India to which for the present their removal can be contemplated. One is Bezwada; the other, Madras. At Bezwada there is no room for them, and it would be useless to go to the expense of building a large building for their reception in such a place. Why not remove them to Madras? As to carriage nothing could be conceived more simple.

From the spot where they lie the ground slopes gently down to the Krishṇá River bank, and the marbles could with the greatest ease be got to the water's edge on rollers. On the east of the Śiva Temple there is an inlet where boats are laden with heavy cargo, and it so happens that the bank at that spot is just so high as to allow cargo at certain seasons of the year to be shipped at the same level direct from the bank into the boats. Engineer officers could so arrange as to embark the marbles direct from the bank into flat punts lying by the side of this inlet without material lifting or lowering. The distance from the Tope may be a quarter of a mile. Once in the punts the marbles could be floated down the river with the stream to Bezwada in a few hours (17 miles). Thence, without transhipment or breakage of bulk, the punts could be towed the entire distance to Madras along the new canal, lately completed and available thanks to the exertions of His Grace the Governor of Madras. There need be no dangerous shipments or voyages by sea. The water communication by canal and river is now open the whole way from Amarávati to Madras. Once there they could be taken to the Central Museum, and would be in a place of safety till the British Museum is ready to receive them, and the necessary funds are forthcoming. At the Central Museum they would probably not be able to be stored under cover in the present building, and it might be necessary to erect a temporary pavilion of iron and wood in which they might be safely kept for the time. Ground is available, I imagine, in the compound of the Museum. Expense there must, of course, be; but it would be trifling considering the advantage derived from the rescue and preservation of these priceless gems of Ancient Indian Art—priceless for the beauty of their sculptures, and for the wealth of the information they contain on all that makes the past history of a nation valuable or interesting to the student, the antiquary, or the statesman.

I am anxious here to tender to Mr. Fergusson my most grateful thanks for repeated acts of kindness and consideration. In spite of the fact that I differ from him in some points, and am so young in the work, he has never refused me the advantage of his advice, assistance, and encouragement.

I am under deep obligation also to Dr. Eggeling, who though personally an entire stranger to me, has with the most disinterested kindness, and at infinite pains, prepared for the Press a transliteration and translation of the Inscription Plate found at the British Museum. Sir Walter Elliot's courtesy, too, has enabled me to add, in an Appendix, some notes on his excavations at Amarávati, which help materially to complete the history of the monument during its last days.

The fortunate discovery in the British Museum of the larger of the two inscription stones drawn by Colonel Mackenzie's clerks in 1816, and since missing, leads to the hope that the more valuable one, the smaller of the two, may possibly at last be found; and that thereby a clue may be obtained to the chronology of the monument.

R. Sewell.

Bonchurch, May 1880.

THE AMARÁVATI TOPE.

§ A.—INTRODUCTION.

It fell to my lot, in the year 1875, to be stationed in the Kistna[1] District of the Madras Presidency, with head-quarters at Bezwada on the Krishṇá River. This is a place of considerable antiquity, once the capital city of the small kingdom of Veṇgi, and afterwards one of the chief towns of the Eastern Chalukyas. The town is surrounded with granite hills honeycombed with the solid rock-cut memorials of ancient religious fervour, and stands on alluvial soil, under which, whenever disturbed, appear the vestiges of past greatness, statues and walls and sculptures of old temples long since fallen and now lying buried under many feet of river silt. Opposite, across the river, is the great four-storeyed temple of Uṇḍavilli, hewn in the solid rock; while in the neighbourhood almost every village has its especial relics of the past, Buddhist or Brahmanical. Here and there are the remains of the circular *stupas* which the followers of the great Reformer erected over relics either of himself or his principal disciples; and 17 miles westward, on the south bank of the river, lie the remains of the most magnificent Buddhist monument in all India—the Amarávati Tope.

The more I looked about me the more it became plain that in a small way I might be of use to Oriental Archæologists by calling attention to remains hitherto unknown, and carrying on work at localities known but only partially investigated; in fact, by humbly following in the footsteps of Mr. J. A. C. Boswell, the late Collector of the District, whose archæological researches had produced such good fruit, but whose lamented death had for the time put such a sudden stop to investigations into the antiquities of the neighbourhood. Accordingly in March of that year I addressed a letter to the Government of Madras, which resulted in my being entrusted by the Government of India with a grant of 1,000 rupees for explorations at Amarávati, Bezwada, Uṇḍavilli, and other places. This was in June 1876. During the close of that year, and the beginning of 1877, I was occupied at the occasional intervals that I could snatch from official business in excavating the Uṇḍavilli Cave Temple. The great famine was then beginning to make itself felt in earnest, and crime was largely on the increase, so that it was not till May 1877 that I found myself able to visit Amarávati and begin work there. Even then there were hindrances. I was greatly pressed for time, the heat was intense, and I was unwell; but, in spite of this, I was successful beyond all expectation in the work accomplished so far as it went. The illness I was suffering from drove me to England on three months' leave in the following July, and on my return to India I was posted, on special duty connected with the famine, to another District. There I found time to write up my First Report on the Antiquities of the Krishṇá, which I submitted in December 1877 to the Government of Madras.

At the commencement of that paper I wrote as follows:—

"4. My present Report is devoted solely to the Uṇḍavilli Cave, the Bezwada Antiquities, and Buddhist remains in the neighbourhood. I leave the entire question of Amarávati to a future occasion for several reasons. I have no skilled draughtsman by me to make exact fair copies of the rough plans and sections I have been able to make myself, and without such plans and sections a notice of the excavations would be useless. I am at a distance from Amarávati, and, having made my notes seven months

---

[1] So styled officially.

ago in pencil on rough pieces of paper, and then become too ill to complete the work satisfactorily, I dare not publish them, for fear of mistakes occurring, till I have carefully gone over the ground again. Moreover, the illustrative photographs that have been taken are so poor as to be almost valueless, and I am very anxious that Government should allow me the services of a better trained man from Madras. For all these reasons I hesitate about publishing my notes till I am in a position to send in a more satisfactory Report. Amarávati is such an important subject that absolute accuracy is essential. . . .

"11. . . . I would earnestly request the Government to grant me the services of a skilled draughtsman. What is wanted is absolute accuracy, and my untrained hand is quite unequal to the task of drawing such careful survey-sketches as are essential to the subject. I would also earnestly beg that a competent photographer may be permitted to visit Amarávati at Government cost and take really valuable photographs of the marbles; worthy of being multiplied for distribution to those gentlemen in Europe who are watching with great interest the result of these explorations;—or, if the Government should so please, for publication. The specimens of photography submitted with this (the best I could get in the neighbourhood, economy being forced on me by the small amount of money at my disposal) are clearly unworthy of the subject in hand.

"12. I submit some of these with this Report, more as protests than as illustration, begging that the Government will be pleased to help me to make the excavations really of use to those at home, by being illustrated in a more satisfactory manner. Amarávati is an impossible place to get at, but its monument is of world-wide interest; and I would strongly urge that a little extra expense should not be allowed to prevent the only method being adopted by which Oriental Scholars and Archæologists can derive benefit from the new discoveries."

"13. I would point out that both draughtsman and photographer ought to be on the spot while the excavations are in progress; the one to take measurements, and mark the position of every marble as it comes to light; the other to stamp in permanence the general progress of the work at its different stages, as well as to afford accurate information on the position of those stones which remain *in situ*. Photographs of separate marbles could be taken afterwards."

Early in 1879 I received the order of the Madrás Government on my Report, in which they acknowledged the necessity for "a sufficient staff of surveyors and photo-"graphers for the special work." But the Order was not so much a reply to me as a paper for the information and orders of the Government of India.

I returned to the Kistna District early in 1878, but it seemed to me not only undesirable to do anything at Amarávati till adequate assistance could be granted to me, or some one else deputed for the work fully provided with such assistance; but in itself improper for me to meddle with work deliberately suspended pending Government Orders. I therefore made no attempt to recommence work at Amarávati during that year.

When I received the order in question early in 1879 I found that the Government of Madras, admitting the necessity for skilled aid, had laid the matter before the Government of India. My hands were therefore tied. Two months later I was invalided home for 18 months.

I mention all these details to show my reasons for delay, and the exact position in which I stood. I was awaiting orders, and was unwilling to proceed with work at Amarávati till that work could be done in a way satisfactory to Archæologists.

On February 26th, 1880, I received a letter from a friend in the Kistna District, stating that His Grace the Duke of Buckingham and Chandos had visited Amarávati and given instructions that the entire remains were to be excavated forthwith,[1] and it is therefore my duty to report without delay all that I know about the Amarávati Tope. If the information as to His Grace's orders is correct this Report will be simply the winding up of my connection with the Tope; if incorrect it will do no harm, and I shall, it

[1] Since writing the above I have been favoured with the inspection of a demi-official communication from Madras which confirms the report I heard privately.

may be, have the satisfaction of revising it hereafter on the spot. And without assuming to myself knowledge I do not possess, it is perhaps no very great presumption on my part to think that the information herein contained may possibly be of use to those engaged on the work, as they may like to know what has been already done. Even though part (Section F.) of this present paper is, to my great regret, only an amplification of notes in many places imperfect, which I had previously withheld because it seemed undesirable to print anything till I could speak decisively on all points, it is clear to me that my duty in the present state of affairs is to state, and state without delay, whatever I happen to know. The information that I possess, imperfect though it is, may do good and can do no harm, so long as my position is thoroughly understood. If permitted by Government to have any share in the work in the future, I shall go over all this ground again as I had originally intended to do. If not, others will doubtless correct me when in error, and complete my labours when imperfect.

The object to be aimed at by any person engaged in excavating these marbles should, I think, be to fix so conclusively the position of each separate stone as it lay imbedded in the soil at Amarávati, that, whether they are transported to Madras or to London or remain exposed where they fell, those interested in the subject and possessing the requisite scientific knowledge may be able to reconstruct the original monument, at least so far as the present position of the remains may enable them to do so. The removal of some stone by one not possessing the requisite knowledge of the scientific importance attaching to the position in which it was found may possibly destroy for ever all chance of determining some valuable or interesting question at present doubtful.

This paper pretends to be nothing more than a description of what I saw at Amarávati, and what I find in Colonel Mackenzie's manuscripts in the Library of the India Office and in some other previous publications, with the deductions which it appears to me necessary to draw from those sources. All my explorations were carried on with the aid of Mr. Fergusson's "TREE AND SERPENT WORSHIP," and it needs no words of mine to express the profound gratitude felt by the Scientific World to the unremitting toil and exertions of that great scholar. If I differ from him in some points it is with the greatest diffidence, and not because I aspire to set up my opinion against his. It appears to me indeed absolutely impossible to avoid differences of opinion on some matters of detail, but the expression of them can only lead to good result by stimulating further inquiry and research on the part of those best able to decide the questions at issue.

Mr. Fergusson's "TREE AND SERPENT WORSHIP," being the standard work on the Amarávati Tope, I shall have to be perpetually referring to it; and to avoid repetition and save space shall call it simply "F." Roman numerals indicate Mr. Fergusson's plates, Arabic the pages of his letterpress.

---

§ B. AMARÁVATI, AND NOTICES OF THE TOPE BY WRITERS PRECEDING MR. FERGUSSON.

Amarávati lies on the south bank of the Krishṇá river, 62 miles from its mouth. A large tract of country in the neighbourhood belonged in the last century to a wealthy Zemindar who resided at Amarávati. In 1797 Colonel Mackenzie, hearing that some finely sculptured stones were to be seen at Amarávati, visited the place and found a number of the marbles *in situ*, but learnt that the Rájah had lately seriously injured the monument by utilizing its materials for the repairs of the handsome Temple to Śiva close by, on the bank of the river. In 1816 and 1817 Col. Mackenzie returned to the spot and prepared careful plans and sketches of the place, with drawings of several of the sculptures, and sent them to the principal museums. They however attracted little attention as no description was sent with them. In 1840 Sir Walter Elliot excavated a number of marbles and sent them to Madras. These were subsequently transmitted to England and are now at the British Museum. Since then the monument has remained *in statu quo*, Mr. Boswell of the Madras Civil Service, late Collector of the District, being the only gentleman who directed public attention to the remains still in existence on the spot.

Occasionally, when any of the European officers of the District visited the place and expressed interest in the subject, the village officers would unearth one or two sculptured slabs for his inspection, and after his departure the shepherd boys and idle lads would set to work to chip and disfigure them as far as lay in their power. This state of things lasted till I commenced excavations systematically in 1877.

It will be interesting, before proceeding to an account of these recent excavations, to know exactly what had been previously written about the monument up to the time when Mr. Fergusson brought it lastingly to notoriety by the publication of his great work. We shall then have an insight into the successive stages of demolition which the monument has undergone since 1796, whilst the extracts which will now be reprinted, and which afford very reliable information on the original shape of the central structure, will I think irresistibly drag the reader to a conclusion on this matter different to that arrived at by Mr. Fergusson.

The earliest notice that I can find is a MS. copy by a clerk of a note apparently by Colonel Mackenzie himself. Mr. Fergusson quotes from it on p. 166 (*note* 2.) and I now give it at length. Colonel Mackenzie had pencilled on it "1798," but had erased that date and written "1803" against it. It is pasted into Mackenzie's volume of the Amarávati sculpture drawings in the India Office Library.

"Memorandum of Amrésvaram in Guntoor, &c.

"To the southwards of the village, close to it, is a circular mound of about 90 feet in diameter which had been cased round with bricks of a large size and slabs of white stone, sculptured so far as I could see by their remains there; for the best stones were carried into the Pagoda which Vassa Reddy was repairing in 1778. Mr. Sydenham took a drawing for me of the fragments that remained; the circular mound is called Dipal-denna or the Hill of Lamps; proceeding from this place North to the South gate of the square Inclosure of the Pagoda lay a slab of white stone, but now grey with the crust of ages; five or six figures are on it sitting apparently on chairs the whole very dim, but a drawing would be desirable.[1]

"The most curious and most complete is to be found further on, close to the outside walls of

[1] I have been unable to identify this marble with any found at Amarávati. Possibly it was removed.

the Pagoda Inclosure on the South, on going towards the river;[1] Here is a small Pagoda of the Lingam formed by three rough stone slabs set on end and covered at top by another placed transversely. On this stone is represented the escalade of a Fort; a figure ascending a ladder; another from a turret on the walls shooting an arrow before the Gate of the Place; a figure with a round shield prostrating himself before a Chief seated on an Elephant, and followed by others on horses, Bullocks, &c.

"The whole forms a Groupe of a very different stile from anything observed anywhere else in this Country, and as the Attitudes, Profiles, &c. differs from the common Hindoo stile an exact drawing would be desirable which could be best done, as a Fac Simile by laying common paper oiled over it and tracing off the outlines with a Pencil. In this manner several Inscriptions were copied in Mysore and it is highly probable there might be here Inscriptions to explain them.

"The annexed sketch will show the situation of the several places."

As stated in the note this sketch unfortunately appears to have been lost. And the slab with the representation of a siege has not yet been identified.

In 1807, Colonel Mackenzie communicated a paper to the Asiatic Society of Bengal, which was printed in "Asiatic Researches," vol. ix., p. 272. This is so interesting that I make no apology for reproducing it. Only a short passage, quite unnecessary to print here, is omitted, together with a sheet of drawings which are rough and of little value.

The drawings are those which were taken for Col. Mackenzie by Mr. Sydenham, as stated in the previous extract.

In consequence of notices received at *Ongole,* I determined to call at *Amrésvaram,* to see the antiquities lately discovered there, as the place is near the banks of the *Críshna,* and we could reach the place whither our tents were to be sent, early in the day. I therefore despatched my interpreter Boria, accompanied by some *Bráhmens* and two *Sepahis,* in the evening, to *Amrésvaram,* with directions to make some previous inquiries into the history of the place: and to conciliate the inhabitants; particularly the *Bráhmens,* who are apt to be alarmed on these occasions.

In the morning, before day, we left *Ibrámpattan* by moonlight, and passed along the north bank of the *Críshna.* We observed, a few miles off, a dry but deep *cálava,* or canal, leading off from the river, probably intended for the purpose of cultivation. At daylight, we were in the sandy bed of the river, which seems to be nearly two miles wide, including the islands; and contains no water at present. We ascended the shallow bank to *Amrésvaram.* The temples appear to be new, and are said to have been recently built by the *Chintapelli Rájá* who has fixed his chief residence here, since *Lacshmípuram* was occupied by our troops. A high mud square wall encloses the temples and his houses; and the rest of the place is laid in regular streets, at right angles, in the same manner with his other places of *Lacshmípuram,* &c. A street, going south from a gate of the temple, seems to be 200 feet wide; and an open *choultry* stands in the intersection of four principal streets. I found Boria ready to receive me, attended by some *Bráhmens;* who said that the people here were rather surprised and alarmed, at the approach of Europeans and *Sepahis,* until he assured them, that our object was merely to view the lately discovered ruins. We were then conducted to those remains of antiquity. We found a circular trench, about 10 feet wide, dug about 12 feet deep, into a mass of masonry, composed of bricks of 16 inches square and 4 inches thick. It is probable that this body of masonry did not extend to a greater depth. The central area was still untouched; and a mass of rubbish was thrown outside of the ditch, which prevented any observation of its original state; but I conjecture, that the whole had, previous to its opening, formed a solid circular mound. In this ditch, a white slab lay broken, which still exhibited some figures in relievo, of which Mr. Sydenham took a sketch. Against the outside of the trench were placed three or four slabs, of the same colour, standing, but inclining inwards; on the inside, where these were uncovered, they had no figures, except where the top of one rose above the earth. Without, some sculptures appeared, which lead me to conclude, that these sculptures were exposed on that side to view. From the inquiries of my *Bráhmens* I could obtain no other account, than that this place was called *Dípál-dinna* or the hill of lamps. The *Rájá,* about a year ago, had given orders to remove a large stone, to be carried to the new pagoda, which he was building, when they discovered the brickwork, which induced them to dig up the rest for the buildings. The white stones were then brought to light, and unfortunately broken; at least we could perceive few of them; and though it was said, that some were carried into the temple, the *Bráhmen,* who was admitted, had perceived only some broken pieces. The sculptured stones, observed, were as follows:—

A broken piece, still lying in the ditch, or excavated foundation, on which appeared something like a *Lingam,* or a pillar, rising through what seemed shaped like a desk, but was probably designed

---

[1] There is a little sketch at the side, and a note, "See the place marked *a* in the sketch." This evidently refers to some sketch plan, but I have not succeeded in finding it amongst Col. Mackenzie's drawings.

for an altar; a male figure stood on the left, with its arms disposed as if pouring something on it; but, as the upper part, and what he held, were broken off, this seems doubtful. Near him stood a female, holding a *Chambú*, or pot, on her head, in the Hindu stile. My *Bráhmen* naturally enough concluded, that this represented a female carrying water to assist in the offering to the *Lingam*. The feet of two figures remained on the right, which probably had appertained to two figures in the same attitude on that side. The stone was a white marble, called by the natives *Pál-ráyi* or milk stone.

NEAR it, stood three slabs, inclining inwards against the masonry, which had been dug out. On the side on which they were viewed, no figures were seen; and they were rough and unpolished: it is probable, that they have sculptures on the side still covered with earth; and I have already mentioned, that some designs appeared at the top of one. If the whole of the circle was faced with these slabs, it is to be regretted, that this treasure of antiquity did not fall into better hands.

ON the rubbish above, near these, and belonging to some unfortunately broken, were two pieces of the same white stone; one of these seemed divided into two compartments, by a border, on which three wild hogs running were sculptured: the outline is well designed. The leg of a figure sitting, and the hind leg of a horse, appear above, remaining of the original design. Below the border, the plane was inclined to a lower border: and in the space of about 6 inches, two lines of characters were carved: on cleaning off the dust, the first line appeared very legibly. I have to regret, that the approaching heat prevented my remaining, to copy this inscription in *fac-simile*. Some of the characters are, however, as I believe, faithfully given in the annexed attempt; and I left a *Bráhmen* to transcribe the whole, but his copy was not satisfactory. In the place marked CC, some of the letters seem to resemble those of the *Ceylon* inscription. The other piece contained the head of a horse, and some defaced heads and prominent ornaments.

NEAR the gate of the temple lay a slab, grey with the crust of ages; but of the same white marble. On it, five or six figures appeared, sitting in various attitudes, on what at first sight seemed to be *Lingams*: but upon close examination, their seats resembled our chairs. The most curious, and most complete piece of sculpture, we found, as we returned along the high mud wall of the temple; laid as a roof over a small temple of *Lingam*, of the same materials. It represented the attack and escalade of a fortified place. The principal figure, on an elephant (with the usual attendants, the driver and the fanner), seemed issuing orders: before him, a pedestrian figure, with a round shield, seemed prostrating himself: a graceful figure, at full length, stood close to the gate of a tower, fronting them. The tower, which was octangular, was surmounted by a rounded roof on pillars, of the shape of an *Ambari;* under which an archer was represented, in the act of drawing his bow, and shooting at an assailant, who covers himself with his shield, while mounting the rampart by a ladder: another figure, from behind the rampart, appeared peeping over, and covered by some defensive arms: several horsemen, and a man mounted on a bullock, seemed to support the attack. The town and rampart seem to be of stone, from the lines drawn obliquely to represent the perspective, which, however aukwardly done, was the first attempt of the kind I had observed in Indian sculpture. To whatever age this is to be attributed, we here find an escalade, defence by flanking towers, and their use, and the mode of attack and defence, illustrated by a Hindu sculpture.

WHEN mention of these sculptures was first made to me at *Ongole*, it was hinted, that they contained marks of the worship of the Jains;[1] but nothing of the kind appeared here. Without my mentioning the subject, I found that the same idea prevailed at this place, though my *Bráhmen* could give me no good reason for it; and the account, which he received of the *Jains*, was very obscure: it was said, that they were formerly a powerful people, who contested the sway with the *Bráhmens*.

ON the lower part of the same slab, and divided by a border containing figures of animals, were sculptured four figures of men sitting on chairs, and reclining, in attitudes different from each other, but all significant of a graceful negligence, indicating careless ease. One of them had his hand disposed on his breast, or in the chain which hung from it; another seemed to incline to one side, leaning against his chair, with one leg and thigh thrown over the other, and wanted nothing but a *hooka* to be placed in his hand, to give a complete idea of that languid attitude, in which we sometimes see an Indian throw himself, when satiated with these fragrant steams that overpower and gratify the sense. The chairs were circular, of a cylindrical form, and the back forming half a circle. A number of small lines divided them longitudinally, and seemed to represent cane work. The thrones or seats, represented in other Hindu sculptures, I had never observed before with backs; so that these seem to have another origin. The figures were too small to admit of distinguishing ornaments: the head-dress was round, and not raised so high as those commonly represented on stones.

ON another stone, but uncertain whether belonging to these, was represented the remains of a God, or chief, sitting on a chair, and fanned by a female holding a *choury*. It is well known, that

---

[1] (*Note by Colonel Mackenzie.*) A figure cross-legged has been since discovered on some of the sculptures found there.—C. M.

Hindu princes, sitting in state, were generally thus attended. So CRISHNA RÁJÁ is described, sitting on his royal throne attended by two beautiful women, fanning him according to royal usage.

A HORSE, on another stone, is preceded by a human figure in a flying attitude, remarkable for its graceful outline; but the upper part of both is destroyed.

THE legs of all the figures are more slender and gracefully disposed, than I have observed in any other Hindu figures; nor have they that drapery, which usually marks with rigid observance their costume. Another remarkable trait is the vast number of rings about the feet, resembling those worn by the *lombádi* or *benjári* women. None are observed on the toes or arms.

AFTER all, though this differ widely from the carvings observed on Hindu buildings, it would be rash to draw any conclusion, until an opportunity offers of observing more sculptures collected. A correct drawing of the complete slab, over the temple of *Mahadéo,* would be extremely desirable, and a complete section across the area of *Dípál-dinna* would perhaps exhibit more remains.

I WAS disappointed in not finding anything like the figure of *Jain-deo,* which I had seen at *Calyani.*

In March 1816 Colonel Mackenzie, with a staff of assistants, took up his residence at Amarávati, and commenced those careful drawings and plans which we find in his MS. volume, and of which Mr. Fergusson writes (p. 164), "These were made by his assistants, "Messrs. Hamilton, Newman, and Burke,[1] and are unsurpassed for accuracy and beauty "of finish by any drawings of their class that were ever executed in India." Colonel Mackenzie himself left in August 1816, but the work went on in his absence till the end of 1817.

In 1817 some of the slabs would appear to have been removed and sent away. The difference between the small plan accompanying this Paper (Plate I.) and the large one published by Mr. Fergusson (Plate XLVII.), which in the original is dated "June 1817," shows the work of clearance that had gone on.

On April 7th, 1817, Colonel Mackenzie writes as follows[2]:—

"MEMORANDUM OF ANTIQUITIES, &c.

"*April* 7, 1817.

"1. Including the inscription eleven stones of *Depauldina* were delivered into the charge of Major Cotgrave at Masulapatam, of which number seven have been sent round to Calcutta. The remaining four;—two of which consist of pillars with lions and figures numbered in my sketch 3 and 4 of loose stones a circular stone with beautiful sculptures No. 55, and the large inscription stone, a Fac-Simile of which was sent some time during last year.[3]

"2. The drawings which Anderson had to finish at Amrawatty when I left the place in August last consisted of seven stones, four of which composed the inner range to the south and numbered according to my sketch[4] 23, 24, 25, 26, and the other three Drawings have also their positions marked on the same paper. The Drawings above alluded to were finished by Anderson soon after and delivered to Lieut[t]. Moundford agreeable to the instructions given him.

"3. Of the curiosities which may have been found whilst they were laying open the Mound of Depauldina enquiry should be made with the great Ranny Yerry-Ama, who resides at Amrawutty, as this Lady was said to be in possession of the best part of the effects of the late Rajah, her consort."

. . . .

Then follow notes of other antiquities in the neighbourhood.

The "Asiatic Journal" for May 1823 (vol. xv., p. 464) contains a description, written by Colonel Mackenzie, of Amarávati, the temples there, the "Dípál-dinne," with the treatment thereof by the above said Rajah, the Fort of Dharaṇikóṭa, with the festivals at the Śiva Temple, and other particulars. These are very interesting as giving

---

1 Anderson's name and Barnett's may be added.

2 MS. note pasted into his volume of Drawings in the India Office Library.

3 The sentence ends off thus abruptly, and it is not stated where those four stones are. I am, however, able to state that one of the pillars mentioned is in England, and is depicted in Mr. Fergusson's elevation on Plate LXXV. The other is drawn on Plate XCVIII., but is not in England. In Col. Mackenzie's volume there is no "No. 55." The large inscription stone I recently discovered in the British Museum. It had lain for many years in the India Office Stores, and had not formed part of the marbles at the India Museum. (See the Appendix to this paper.) The small inscription stone is highly necessary to be discovered, and Mackenzie says it was sent to Calcutta. Can it not be found?

4 This sketch, which would have probably been of great value, cannot be found.

detailed descriptions of the place, and showing the matured convictions of the officer whose energy first brought its grandeur into notoriety.

The first extract that I give is concerned merely with the topography of Amarávati and the neighbourhood :—

"RUINS OF AMRAVUTTY, DEPAULDINA, AND DURNACOTTA.

"TOPOGRAPHICAL.

"In giving a description of Amravutty, it is difficult to do justice to the peculiar beauty and grandeur of this celebrated town, as well as to the interesting antiquities of Depauldina, and the vestiges with which Durnacotta and the country in its vicinity abound.

"From these ancient remains, particularly of the former, it naturally inclines one to believe that this place was formerly the residence and capital of a great monarch, distinguished for splendour, opulence, and knowledge, under whose liberal encouragement the art of sculpture had attained to its greatest perfection and excellence, as may be witnessed in the infinite variety of interesting carvings with which Depauldina is furnished.

"But whatever may have been the splendour and extent of Durnacotta in the plenitude of its prosperity, like all other considerable places of antiquity, it had fallen into decay and insignificance, till the building of the town of Amravutty in its neighbourhood, which has in a great measure revived its former fame, by bringing to light one of its most inestimable productions, which otherwise might yet have remained in perfect obscurity.

"As Amravutty, therefore, is the present flourishing capital of the munificent Zemindar Vassareddy, it shall be first treated of.

"This large and populous town is pleasantly situated in a plain, extending along the south bank of the river Kistna, about twenty miles N.N.W. from Guntoor, and twelve miles in a direct line S.W. of the fortress of Condapilly. It is built with some degree of taste and regularity, which bespeak the opulence and grandeur of its founder, who accomplished this object about twenty-three years ago, when this site is said to have contained but a few humble habitations of Bramins and others, adjoining to the ancient temple of Amreshvaran.

"The late Rajah Venkatadry-naid has the reputation of having built this town; under whose encouragement and protection settlers arrived from various places and established themselves. His acts of munificense and amplification of charity are said to have been such, that during his life time the place was the crowded resort of people of various descriptions, particularly Bramins, great numbers of whom used to be entertained at a time, and furnished with money and other presents.

"The streets and lanes of this beautiful town are laid out in straight lines, which run north and south, intersected at right angles by others extending east and west. The figure of the town considered, not including its suburbs on the south, and the four streets which project on the west, is of a rectangular shape, measuring 615 by 450 yards, but inclusive of the other component parts just noticed, its extent would be considerably increased, being in length from north to south, 1175 yards, and in breadth 765 and upwards.

"The grand street extending from the great Pagoda of Amreshvar towards Ramalingam on the south, forms the only market of the place; it is 100 feet in breadth, and the bazars which are on each side appear rather low, having flat roofs, which are covered with earth. The next principal street is the one which leads from the square tank of Shevagunga, westerly. It is 30 feet wide, the projecting part of which in this direction constitutes the Agrar for Bramins. It is in length 300 yards, and the houses on both sides are remarkable for their uniformity, being raised two stories.

"The western side, which forms the largest proportion of the town, is chiefly inhabited by Bramins; they are said to be rich from being in the Zemindar's employ, and the houses here consequently make the most agreeable appearance, consisting chiefly of two stories, the roofs of which, like the other dwellings situated in the regular part of the town, are covered with tiles. The eastern side, however, is less shewy: it is where the mechanics, artificers, and others of this denomination reside.

"The suburbs joining on with the south end of the town extend east of Ramalingam pagoda. They contain a great many streets and lanes, which, however, are rather irregular; the houses in this part are constructed of earth, and covered with thatch, which form the habitations of the lower class of natives; of a similar construction are the dwellings which lie west of Depauldina, tenanted by washermen and day-labourers.

"The most remarkable buildings are the several pagodas, the Rajah's palaces, and mosques.

"Of these the great temple of Amreshvar stands at the upper end of the town, on a gently-rising ground, embracing the bank of the river. It is an ancient pagoda of great celebrity, sacred to Sivoo worship; and consists of three enclosures one within another. The outermost enclosure is surrounded by a *chunamed* wall, fifteen feet in height, forming a quadrilateral figure, very irregular, through which are four entrances, but that to the south is distinguished from the rest by having a lofty spire. The walls which encompass the two inner enclosures are built of masonry; the principal entrance into those recesses is from the eastern side. Along the outside of the second enclosure-wall to the south, is a line of accommodation for spectators at public festivals; the whole length 230 feet by 13 broad: the roof is terraced and supported by a row of wooden pillars. On the eastern side is a similar construction.

"The principal sanctuary lies in the inmost enclosure; part of the roof of which in front is adorned with small statues of copper richly gilt, and the high spire which rises exactly over the sacred recess is highly gilt, surmounting a ball of the same appearance.

"Besides the Amreshvar there are several smaller pagodas sacred to other deities contained within the enclosures, the pyramidal roofs of all of which have likewise ornamental work of copper doubly gilt, which, by their lustre, certainly add to the diversifying beauty and grandeur of the place.

"At the distance of 655 yards southward of the above is the temple dedicated to Ramalingan-Swamy, which is seated on a gently-rising ground contiguous to Depauldina. A mud wall of a modern height surrounds it. The enclosure measures 270 feet in length by 132 in breadth, within which, besides the pagoda, is a handsome Muntapun with stone columns, and near it on a pedestal is a beautiful pillar 25 feet high, entirely composed of plates of copper richly gilt. There is no annual celebration in honour of this pagoda, but daily worship is regularly observed. It is a modern erection by the late Rajah Venkatadry naid, and has an inscription to that effect, the date whereof is Sallivan Sheca, or A.D. 1735."

Then follows a description of the Mussulman mosques and buildings, the Rajah's mahals and gardens, which I omit; passing on to Colonel Mackenzie's account of the Dharaṇikóṭa Fort:—

"At the distance of 500 yards from the western end of the town of Amravutty, is situated Durnacotta, which is said to have been the ancient capital of this part of the country, under the government of Molcuntymaharaze, and was also his residence. The vestiges of this ancient fort denote that it has been a place of some strength, the walls appear amazingly thick, and of considerable elevation. Its form is that of a square but somewhat irregular to the north, the space between which and the Kistna is adorned with small gardens. The embankments on this side are also much higher, and divided by nullahs which run into the river. The dimensions of each side of the fort are about 630 yards. The gateways appear to have stood opposite each other, in eastern and western directions. The quantity of bricks that are said to have been dug up, and the abundance of small pieces with which the excavations are filled, give every reason to suppose that it was a brick construction, the walls of which appear to have been about 25 feet in thickness. The surface of the ground within is very uneven; in one part in particular, where the nullah takes his passage, the slopes on either side of it are very considerable.

"A road passing through the fort, in a direction from east to west, may be considered as forming a grand street. The portion lying north of it is entirely filled with houses, and contains a few fine streets. Of the southern portion, part to the east is occupied with houses, but the greater share lies waste, exhibiting a very uneven and stony surface. The houses are constructed of mud, and have all thatched roofs, save a few belonging to Bramins, which are covered with tiles. Those that reside in Durnacotta are chiefly husbandmen of the tribe Cummawars and Buljewars; there are besides a few other casts, some of which also follow the same occupation.

"From the south-east angle of the fort an embankment extends eastward to the new garden; another runs at right angles with it on the north: the space included forms the site of Noonabgoondum, of which tradition says that it was a famous reservoir in ancient times. The site of Humshagoondum is shown near the house in the southern portion. It is almost filled up with earth washed down from the contiguous heights. Above Noonabgoondum, as well as to the east of it, are shady topes of tamarind trees: of the latter a great part has been cut down for fuel for the use of the Zemindar. The tope appears to have occupied a large area, and from its affording a very shady retreat, had received the name of Checkady-Wunnum, or the dark grove.

"To the southward of Durnacotta the ground is high and stony, resembling hally-land. Some vestiges of antiquity are here perceivable, but that of Nuckadeverdinna, which lies furthest south, is the most entire. It is a circular mound of earth rising to a moderate height, and thirty feet in diameter: above it are some places which have been opened for bricks. The temple Butsulammah is situated on the highest part: it is a neat stone building of ancient date, sacred to the Sacti worship, whose name it bears.

"The ancient city of Durnacotta is said to have extended $3\frac{1}{4}$ miles in length; on the west to the village of Mootipollian, and on the east to the small pagoda of Pedentyammen, in the road to Vycoontapoor. These places are each about $1\frac{3}{4}$ miles from the centre of Durnacotta. On the south the extent is not precisely known, but it is supposed it did not extend beyond Nuckadeverdinna. Within the space described of the ancient city, I have been informed that, in several places along the banks of the river, bricks were found, as well as rings of potters-ware, with which wells were constructed.

"About a mile westward of Durnacotta are some singular antiquities, a number of which are seen on the cultivated heights in circles formed by stones, taken from the large masses of rock contiguous to them. These circles are very ancient, and appear to be similar to those of the Puncha-Pandawars.—In number they are about 17 or 18: the smaller measure in diameter 25 feet, the larger 32. The stones composing these circles are of a hard blackish granite, very irregular in their shape, and in general measuring in height about three feet, and about the same in thickness. The country people are entirely ignorant of the subject of these antiquities, and can give no information for what purposes they were designed. It is reported that circles of a similar description are very numerous among the skirts of the hills of Wudlamaun, and others in that neighbourhood, situated a few coss to the south-eastward of Amravutty: that on some of these being opened by the late Rajah Vassareddy Venkatadry-naid, they were found to contain human bones of a larger size than the skeletons of men of the present day, and that in others there were earthen pots curiously placed together, containing ashes, &c., &c."

Those desirous of studying maps or plans of the localities above described will find a sufficient one in F., XLVI., which is copied from Colonel Mackenzie's MS. volume.

The next extract from Mackenzie's paper is highly interesting and important:—

"Description of the Antiquities of Depauldina.

"The mound of Depauldina lies close to the southern skirts of the town, and from the interesting remains of antiquity there, claims particular attention.

"At the depth of 10 feet from the top of the mound, stones, with a variety of sculptures, are seen, which are ranged in two circles, one within the other,—the space between them is 13 feet, paved so far as it is entire with large slabs of slate stone. The diameter of the inner circle measures 166 feet. It is difficult to say what the area included within this space originally contained. It is evident that it was in later times intended to be formed into a reservoir, which its present state fully exhibits, but was left unfinished. On the south side, within the circles, a strong work of masonry is discernible, which may probably be the remains of an interior wall, as the people of the village informed me that a similar work had been observed all round, which has since been cleared away in removing the earth. This mysterious structure is supposed to have four entrances; that only to the south has lately been cleared, which is 25 feet within, but becomes narrower as it recedes outward.

"The order in which the sculptures are placed is very regular. They are disposed according to the work they possess;—Those with pretty large figures form the exterior range; they are a foot in thickness, and nearly three broad, and rise six or seven feet high. Between every two entire stones are placed two of a circular form one above the other, having a small projecting rim at each end, fixed into grooves made on either side of the adjoining stones. These circular stones do not rest upon one another, there is a space between them of two or three inches, and the same may be observed at the bottom; they are not on a level with the base of the adjoining stones. The length of the grooves is according to the dimensions of the stones inserted;—they are two inches apart, at the extremities an inch or little more in breadth: in the middle of the breadth is five or six inches, and three deep.

"The lower circular stones are finished with carvings resembling foliage, and those placed above display a variety of figures in bas-relief. The same observation may be extended to the adjoining stones, with the exception, however, that the lower part of them is semicircular representing foliage, under which is a border with flowers and figures of lions.

"The slabs composing the inner circle are remarkable for the beauty of the sculptures upon them, which are small, and consist of figures, festoons, and a variety of ornaments, very neatly executed. On the sides are pillars, which are finished either with figures of lions and horses, or of men and women; and over the top is an entablature replete with figures in various acts of devotion or amusement. These inner slabs have been cemented to each other with strong mortar, and supported by a wall of masonry rising to a moderate height in the rear; the adjustment has been very happily executed. Some of these slabs are six inches in thickness, and others nearly nine inches: their shape is chiefly rectangular. All the carvings appear originally to have been painted red and varnished; and so fine was the composition used, that the stones still retain part of the ancient colouring, which, from the length of time they have laid under ground, is now somewhat faded, inclining to a copperish red.

"Upon a minute inspection of the several sculptures, in many a story is completely told, with clearness and precision, and the characters accurately defined. The passions also are naturally exhibited and strongly marked; and exactness of outline in the representation, as well as in the air and carriage of animals, is happily delineated, and the festoons, foliage, flowers, and an infinite variety of other decorations, which adorn these carvings, are altogether excellent. The artists appear to have been skilled in perspective also; upon the whole, neither taste nor elegance are wanting, and in the article of neat and delicate finishing, the carvings and sculptures of Depauldina are far superior to any ancient or modern Hindoo production.

"A great many slabs, of a large size, are seen lying on the surface of the reservoir, but it is difficult to say where they were originally placed. On these are chiefly represented a few large figures of men and women, in divisions of two or three, one above another, each three feet high. Some of these are well executed, and the proportions are correct.

"A great part of the mound remains uncleared; of the exterior row only the south-east quarter, and the entrance in that direction have been opened. The whole of the inner circle has been dug up, and the stones removed for the purposes of building. They have been chiefly applied in the repair of the pagodas, and a great many are put to form a flight of steps to the square tank of Shevagunga; the site in question is 210 feet long.

"From the extremely careless manner in which the workmen proceeded in opening the mound, scarcely a single stone has escaped uninjured, while a great many have been totally destroyed. The excavation in the centre, intended for a reservoir, is nearly a square, each side of which measures 108 feet; in the middle is a well dug some feet deeper. The intention of digging into the mound, I have been told, originated in a desire of finding treasure, which the late Rajah supposed it contained, and with this view the search was continued, but it was not known whether anything was found in it, with the exception of a large store of bricks, and the stones with sculpture. It was intended to have made the reservoir a hundred yards square; had this been accomplished, every part of the structure underground would have been laid open for inspection.

"In the state the mound is in at present, it is impossible to form any conjecture whether there was any, and what sort of building formerly standing in the centre, or for what purpose it was intended. But if any opinion may be formed barely from the sculptures that are represented, it would appear to have been a place consecrated to religious worship, but by a different sect from the Hindoos of the present day, as there are none of the mythological figures to be seen among the numerous sculptures to warrant a supposition in favour of the Braminical devotion. The ancient name of the place was Doop Mogasallah;[1] which appellation it derived, according to tradition, from its having been the place where the ancient sovereign Mookuntymaharaze held his Durbar, and where he used to transact business of state.

"There is not a doubt but that some erection has stood in the centre, from the immense quantities of broken bricks with which the spaces between the two rows of stones are everywhere filled. The mound of earth must have been raised in later times, to prevent the total destruction of the invaluable stones; or, perhaps, the policy of those concerned in introducing a new system of religion, the better to effect their purpose, and prepare the minds of the people to embrace their doctrines, may have deemed it expedient to conceal from the votaries a place sacred to their ancient modes of worship.

"If the surrounding embankment was cleared, the inner surface, where the stones are placed, would evidently appear to be on the same line of level with the adjacent ground. Another reason for supposing that the earth was raised in later times, is from the circumstance that the exterior range of stones possesses sculptures and carvings on the back part also, which, had they been intended to be placed against an embankment, there would have been no necessity for this additional adornment, which was to be concealed from view."

"A Descriptive Memorandum.

"At the period when Mokunty aharaze (*sic*) held the sovereignty of the Joyathee country, he erected close to the eastern side of the capital a circular structure, surrounded with slabs of exquisite sculptures, where he used to transact business of state, and the place in consequence derived the appellation of Doop Mogasalla; but the modern name by which it is at present distinguished is Depauldina, or the luminous height.

"About twenty-three years ago (S. S. 1718) the Rajah Vassareddy Venkatadry Naid, Zemindar.

---

[1] (*Note by Mackenzie.*) Mogasallah, in the Tellinga language, signifies a court for public affairs, and the distribution of justice. What the word "doop" signifies I could obtain no explanation. I should suppose it to be a word of Moorish, or Sanscrit derivation denoting sun, sunny court, from being in the open air without any shelter. It may not be improbable that Depauldina served for the same purpose, and owed its origin to the same religion as the circles of the Druids, which were solar temples, and where also all assemblies were held, for public deliberation and the distribution of justice. In some other parts of Europe they are distinguished by appropriate names, denoting judicial circles; and history further informs us, that the Druids always opened their meetings for civil affairs with acts of religion: so it might have been here, and the sculptures represented are well calculated for this purpose, to inculcate on the minds of the people such moral and religious lessons as to dispose them to fervent acts of devotion of the deity to whose worship the place has been consecrated. We have additional motives for conjecturing the above from the ancient tumuli which abound in this neighbourhood, and also along the skirts and on the summits of the hills situated within a few miles E. of Amravutty, which are proved to have been the ancient sepulchres, monuments or cemeteries of the dead, from the relics found in them, as bones, &c.

of Chintapilly, after visiting the temple of Amreshwar, proceeded on a religious tour to perform his devotions at the celebrated Pagoda of Tripetty; on his return he felt disposed to change his residence from Chintapilly, and found a new city, so that he pitched upon the scite of Amravutty as the best suited for the purpose, from its contiguity to the Kistna river, the openness of the country around, and the sanctity of its temple, which is reckoned the first among five principal places of Shivoo worship in the country of Tellangana.

"To effect his views, he invited Banians from Chintapilly, Pennagunchyprole, Nundigamah, and Batavole, as well as Bramins and other settlers, to all of whom he made suitable advances of money to enable them to erect habitations. While thus engaged preparing accommodations for himself, the employment suggested to his mind the possibility of obtaining bricks by digging for them in the several mounds of earth with which Durnacotta and the adjacent grounds abounded. With this view he commenced first at Nuckadeverdina, which was then a pretty high circular mound; after digging all round it to the depth of one yard and a half, a few large bricks were all that was found, with broken pieces of the same material somewhat lower. This mound at present measures in diameter thirty feet, and is of moderate height.

"He next directed his search in quest of the same materials to another mound of earth, a little higher up, near Bulsulamma Pagoda, an ancient Sacti temple: on opening which, at the depth of one cubit, a great quantity of entire bricks were collected, and the search in consequence was continued to a greater depth. The excavation at present forms a small receptacle for water supplied by the annual rains. The search was afterwards continued on the western side of the ruinous fort of Durnacotta with similar success.

"While the palace, &c. were yet finishing, the Mussulmen people who had taken up their residence at the south end near Depauldina, in digging for the same purposes, had occasionally found bricks of an extraordinary size as well as a few fragments which possessed beautiful carvings, which circumstance was reported to the Rajah, who eagerly came over to inspect the place, and perceiving that it was the most curious of the several mounds he had caused to be opened, conceived that it might embowel something of value; as most places so marked are generally the receptacles of hidden treasures, he commanded the Mussulmen to move elsewhere, as he designed to form a garden there, and a reservoir in the centre. Soon after this he ordered workmen to be employed in digging the mound of Depauldina, the upper part of which rose in a turreted shape to the height of twenty feet, which was cased round with bricks [1] of unusual dimensions; the diameter at top measured about thirty yards.

"In digging along the eastern skirts of it, a small temple was discovered, near which lay an image which Vassareddy caused to be taken into the temple of Amreshvar, supposed for public worship. A small distance west of the above two pillars were next cleared, which resembled (and perhaps once formed) the entrance to a small pagoda.

"The workmen next proceeded to lay open the western side, in which direction also a small building was discovered, which contained a large pillar lamp in a complete state, having a basin at bottom, and places at top for five wicks or lights. It contained about ten seers of copper, which, on being committed to the fire, dissolved into dross, from its having been very much injured and earth-eaten. On the north side of the mound, where at present extends a line of houses, with that part of it left unoccupied and rather low, a Muntup of four pillars was found, built with bricks; this is supposed to have been a chapel of Jaina worship, from a headless image which it contained sitting cross-legged.

"While forming the reservoir at Depauldina, all the sculptured slabs of various sizes which were found on the northern side were removed to the tank of Shevagunga, with which the flight of steps on the western side, to the number of twenty, was constructed. Some of the remaining stones have been carried into the great pagoda, part of which are placed as steps to the sanctuary of Amreshvar, while some are placed in the wall at the entrance of the pagodas of Mysasoor-Murdanee and Soameshwar. In short these valuable stones of antiquity have been used in various buildings, both public and private; those in particular applied to Mussulmen mosques have first been carefully divested of every carving by rubbing them on harder stones, to prevent, as it is said, any pollution arising to Mahomedan faith from idolatrous substances.

"The koneer or reservoir intended to be formed here was to have measured 100 yards; had this been accomplished, every part of the curiosities contained underground would have been brought to light, and an opportunity thereby afforded of forming a more accurate conception of its extent, design, and the beautiful and interesting specimens of the ingenuity and art of the ancient Hindoos. Since the inroad of the Pindaries, in March 1816, the work of forming the reservoir at Depauldina has

---

[1] (*Note by Mackenzie.*) Length of the bricks 20 inches, 10 in breadth, and 4 thick. Cut straw and leaves appear to have been used in their composition. The earth also of which they have been made must have been potter's earth from the hardness and fineness of the colour.

been discontinued; and the death of the Rajah Venkatadry Naid, which happened in August of the same year, put a period to its completion.

"Since the Rajah established Amravutty as his capital, he made considerable improvements and additions to the great pagoda, by enlarging the area of ground about it, and erecting several new temples, besides which he built the lofty spire over the southern entrance."

In 1832, there is a Paper by H. H. Wilson, in the "Asiatic Researches" (Vol. XVII., pp. 561 and 582, with Plate), on some "Select Coins," in which he incidentally mentions a—

"Collection of the late Colonel Mackenzie, which contained . . . . (*amongst others*) . . . . Roman coins dug up chiefly at Dipaldinna near Amarâvati, near the Godaveri."

Plates and descriptions of two are given, but they are of little assistance. As Mr. Fergusson remarks (p. 170), they are of the Bactrian type. No details of the Roman coins are given, nor do we know where they were discovered. The expression "at Dipaldinna" is too vague to lead to any result.

The next notice that I can find of Amarâvati is the Paper by Prinsep in the "Journal of the Asiatic Society of Bengal," for 1837, (Vol. VI., p. 218) on the two principal inscribed stones. He worked these out only from copies by Colonel Mackenzie's clerks. Mackenzie's memorandum of April 7, 1817, says distinctly that the small inscription stone was sent to Calcutta previous to that date with six other sculptured marbles. For, of the eleven stones mentioned, seven were "sent round to Calcutta;" and the other four are described, one of which is "the large inscription stone," but not the small one. The small inscription, then—the stone of all others most necessary to discover for its possible historical allusion—*vide* General Cunningham's Note to Inscription IX. (F., Appendix E., p. 261), and Mr. Fergusson on p. 168—may all this time be at Calcutta. Perhaps General Cunningham may be able to help us in this direction?

Prinsep gives translations and transliterations of the two stones, but it is not advisable here to waste space by reproducing his remarks. In the present state of scientific research any speculations founded on admittedly faulty copies made by inexperienced hands would at once be rejected.

But I may remark that the general form of the characters on the later, *i.e.*, the longer inscription, would not appear to be of later date than the eighth century, and that Mr. Fergusson's deduction (p. 171, *note* 5) as to Buddhism being in a flourishing state in the twelfth century would hardly be justified merely by the letters of this inscription.[1]

In Wilson's "Ariana Antiqua," published in 1841 (pp. 32, 33), there is a short notice of Amarâvati, which it is unnecessary to reproduce. But one passage is important. He writes:—

"Several of the sculptured slabs were brought away by him (Colonel Mackenzie), and *some of them are now in the Museum of the Asiatic Society of Bengal,* and in that of the East India Company."

This confirms the conjecture founded on Mackenzie's MS. One of those stones is the valuable *small inscription stone*.

I can find no detailed account of what number of stones Colonel Mackenzie deported to Masulipatam, beyond the mention given above of the eleven entrusted to Major Cotgrave. But from a Report on the slabs at the Central Museum, Madras, furnished by the Rev. William Taylor to the Government of Madras, and published in "Selections from the Records of the Government of Madras," 1856, Vol. XXXIX., I learn that in 1830 Mr. Robertson, then Collector of Masulipatam, who was laying out a new market-place in the quarter of that town which still bears his name,—"brought down some of the Amarawaty sculptures and placed them in the square of the market-place"—to beautify it.

And in 1835, Dr. Benza, publishing his journal of a tour, during which he visited Masulipatam,[2] in Vol. V. of "The Madras Journal of Literature and Science," writes as follows:—

"In the middle of the Pettah,[3] at the spot where the two principal streets cross each other, are

---

[1] Since writing the above I have been fortunate enough to discover this slab in the British Museum, and am enabled to append to this paper a facsimile from the marble (*Plate IV.*), and notice of it (*Appendix*).

[2] On January 16th, 1835.

[3] Suburb or quarter of a large village or town.

placed erect and arranged in a circular form, thirty-three large slabs of a compact limestone covered with numerous figures in *basso* and *alto relievo*, of the most exquisite execution, excelling any in the few places I have visited in India, containing such relics of the remotest antiquity, the Seven Pagodas not excepted. The sculptures at Masulipatam, being cut in compact limestone, of a very fine texture are susceptible of receiving a delicacy, a kind of mellowness in the execution of figures and friezes, which it is impossible to impart to the coarse grained pegmatitic rock of the Seven Pagodas. There is such anatomical correctness in these figures, and so much nature and freedom in their positions and attitudes, that Gaggino [1] himself would have been proud of acknowledging them as his work.

"These sculptured slabs were brought from the ruins of a Pagoda seven miles from Masulipatam; [2] and by what I remarked in one of them, they must have belonged to a more ancient building than the Pagoda whence they were brought to Masulipatam. One of the largest slabs (more than four feet high) had one of the two surfaces, convex, the other plane. On the convex one were multitudes of figures which covered its whole space, representing processions, sacrifices (?) of animals, and other religious ceremonies, said to be those of the *Jain* tribe. On the back surface was sculptured a reversed column, the pedestal turned upwards, and the capital downwards; showing that the two faces of the stone had been sculptured and used at two different periods, and for two different buildings." [3]

"Among the sculptures at Masulipatam there was a piece, apparently part of the entablature of an architrave, which was really in a very refined style; there were figures of lions, tigers, rhinoceroses, buffaloes, and men executed with so much taste and so exquisitely correct, as to call forth the admiration of all who saw it.

"This, and many others of the sculptures, attracted the Right Honourable the Governor's attention; who, on the spot, gave orders for their transmission to a safer, cleaner, and more conspicuous place."

A note states that, up to the time of publication, these slabs had "not yet reached their destination, the Museum of the Literary Society." From Mr. Taylor's Report in 1857 they would appear to have been sent down by Mr. Goldingham a ta later period.

This was in 1835. In 1840 Sir Walter Elliot, then Commissioner of Guntoor, 20 miles from Amarávati, carried down to Madras a considerable number of the marbles, which Mr. Fergusson states (p. 163) had been built into the walls of a "little chapel" just at the side of the Tope. Most unfortunately Sir Walter Elliot's notes and papers were destroyed in their passage to England, and it is probable that that gentleman would be unable to distinguish from memory, amongst the marbles now in our possession, those that were at Masulipatam previous to his excavations at Amarávati, and those which he brought from Amarávati himself. We thus have a considerable confusion, the marbles excavated by Colonel Mackenzie, by Mr. Robertson, and by Sir Walter Elliot being mixed up together.

In 1854, Dr. Balfour, in a Report on the Government Central Museum (published in the "Selections from the Records of the Madras Government," 1854, No. II.), mentioning the collection of different kinds of marble [3] found in the Presidency, states that—

"the value of some of them, for purposes of sculpture, may be ascertained by making an examination of the collection of basso relievos lying in front of the Museum, which Mr. Walter Elliot brought to Madras from Amrawaty about 14 years ago" (p. 11);

and subsequently (p. 22) catalogues as No. 19 of a geological collection of specimens of marble from the Masulipatam district:—

"A Buddhist pillar or slab of the Juggiapettah marble broken in two. The sculpture represents four different subjects;"

and he then accurately describes one of the inner enclosure side pillars (*i.e.*, one of the side

---

[1] The celebrated Sicilian sculptor in *basso* and *alto relievo*.

[2] Altogether erroneous. Amarávati is 60 miles from Masulipatam.

[3] This slab is still at Masulipatam, or was when I left that place to return to England early in April 1879. It is one of the inner enclosure Dagobas, and is in magnificent preservation.

[4] The marble of which these sculptures are composed is generally called "*Palnád marble*," from the tract of country so called commencing about 30 miles west of Amarávati. The name "Palnád" itself is evidently derived from the words "*Pālu-nāḍu*," milk-country," large tracts of land there being almost paved with this marble.

pillars of the various groups of three which occupy the spaces between the Dagobas). This pillar was drawn by Burke for Colonel Mackenzie in 1816, and is No. 22*b* of his MS. collection, but it is not in England. This is remarkable; for if it was at Madras it ought now to be in London, only two portions of an outer rail pillar now remaining at the Madras Museum. Other sculptured marbles are mentioned in Dr. Balfour's lists.

In 1857 was published by the Madras Government a further Report on the Madras Museum (Vol. XXXIX.), in which (Appendix B., p. 195) the Rev. William Taylor gives an elaborate account of the Amarávati marbles then at Madras. It is useful as giving here and there details concerning the recovery of the marbles, but his speculations on chronology, &c. must be distrusted. Later research has proved them to be absolutely valueless. About the same time was published a handsome volume of photographic illustrations of the marbles then at Madras, by Captain Tripe, of the Madras Army.

Mr. Taylor writes (p. 220) that there were originally 90 marbles sent by Sir Walter Elliot to Madras 14 years previously, but "there are others since arrived (during the month of April) from Masulipatam." This probably refers to April 1855 or 1856. Commencing on p. 249 he gives a detailed account of these newly arrived ones, and there appear to have been 39 of them. It is not stated who sent them, but we may conjecture that they were sent from Masulipatam by Mr. Goldingham.[1]

On p. 224 Mr. Taylor gives us a summary of the contents of a Telugu document found amongst the Collection of Mackenzie MSS., containing an account of the Journey in 1817 of one Ananda Rao (one of Colonel Mackenzie's collectors) in the Districts about Amarávati, and his work there under Mr. Hamilton's orders, which account Prinsep had referred to in his Paper in 1823 on the two inscribed stones (*see above*) regretting that he could not lay his hands on it. From this it appears that on February 16th, 1817, Ananda Rao—

> "had a large white marble slab lying at Dharana Cota carefully scoured and whitewashed. The two following days he copied off the inscriptions on it fully, and gave the transcript to Mr. Hamilton, who said he would send it to Madras."

Possibly this is the larger of the two inscriptions published by Prinsep, the stone, according to the measurement given in Colonel Mackenzie's MS. copy, being 5 feet high. But if so Mr. Taylor's statement that it was found not at the Amarávati Tope, but at the Fort of Dharaṇikóṭa close by is erroneous, for the original facsimile pasted in Colonel Mackenzie's volume is distinctly stated to be a "Reduction of an Ancient Inscription on stone found in *Depaldinna*," and his plan places it on the north side of the circle.

Sir Walter Elliot, in his Paper on the Coins of Southern India, published in Vol. XIX. of the Madras Journal (p. 225), incidentally mentions that the marbles at the Madras Museum came from Amarávati, but goes into no details.

The above are all the notices that I can trace concerning Amarávati and its marbles, published antecedent to Mr. Fergusson's great work on "Tree and Serpent Worship."

About the year 1856 the bulk of the marbles arrived in England, and as Mr. Fergusson tells us were stowed away in the coach-house of Fife House till discovered by him in 1867. Their importance was at once recognized, and shortly after appeared the first edition of his invaluable work.

This splendid volume is open to the public, but Colonel Mackenzie's MS. folio is not, and it is incumbent on me to give what publicity I can to the matters contained in it which more especially assist in the elucidation of the history of the monument.

---

[1] 90+39=129. Two outer rail pillars still remain at Madras. I imagine, though there is little to guide us, that the remaining 127 marbles were sent to England. It will be shown below that only 18 of these are Mackenzie's. 109 must be Sir Walter Elliot's and Mr. Robertson's.

§ C. EXCAVATIONS AT AMARÁVATI PREVIOUS TO 1877.

THE MS. volume of drawings and plans connected with Amarávati collected by Col. Mackenzie contains, first, two maps and three sheets of plans and sections. The first of the maps is Mr. Fergusson's Plate XLVI., the scale, 1 inch to a mile, being retained.[1] The second is an enlarged map, on a scale of 4 inches to a mile. This it is unnecessary to reproduce as it teaches little more than can be gathered from the other, except that it localizes the "Shevagunga Tank" where many marbles may be expected to be found, but of whose very existence I was all along ignorant. The Tank is situated on the east side of the village, and a flight of steps belonging to it are stated by Colonel Mackenzie to contain many of the sculptured slabs belonging to the Tope. Whether this tank is now in existence or not I cannot say, for though I was several times at Amarávati, no-one directed my attention to it; and as it is not marked on the plan published by Mr. Fergusson I concluded that the name "Śivagangá" had been applied by the Chintapalli Rajah to the tank hollowed out at the Tope itself. In Mr. Fergusson's plan (XLVI.) it is indicated by a small square on the east of the village, but in Colonel Mackenzie's plan this little square is coloured blue, which would sufficiently identify it as a reservoir for water.

The first of Colonel Mackenzie's two plans is deserving of attention for several reasons, and I make no apology for reproducing it (Plate I., accompanying this paper). It will be seen, first, that it records an earlier stage of the Tope than that perpetuated in the second plan (published by Mr. Fergusson, Plate XLVII.). The description of the first is "Sketch of Deepauldinna at Amrawutty *in its present state, March* 1816." Col. Mackenzie's own description appended to the second, but not printed by Mr. Fergusson, is "Plan descriptive of the present state of the mound of Depaldenna at Amravutty, shewing what has been cleared out and what still remains to be removed. Laid down from actual measurements, *June 1817*."[2] (The italics are mine.)

The small plan depicts 20 stones of the inner circle, and 21 of the outer, in position on the south-east of the mound, declaring that 14 of the latter had been "drawn by Newman." But amongst the 75 drawings of sculptures in the Mackenzie Collection there is not one that is noted as having been "drawn by Newman," though almost all bear the initials of other copyists. It would be extremely desirable to procure these 14 drawings, as the localisation of the marbles would thereby be greatly facilitated.

It is noticeable that the position of stones in the small plan differs to some extent from that of the larger one, and I am afraid there is no clue to a solution of this difficulty. But the small plan is especially interesting for two reasons.

In the large plan is a hitherto unexplained broad pink band on the south-west of the circle, inside the rails but concentric with them, its external boundary being 12 feet from the inside of the inner enclosure. This is seen in the small plan with the additional help of measurements. It was 40 feet long and 8 feet broad.

Now, amongst the extracts already given from Colonel Mackenzie's description of Amarávati and the Depaldinna, will have been noticed the following passage:—

> "On the south side, within the circles, a *strong work of masonry* is discernible, which may probably be the remains of an interior wall, as the people of the village informed me that *a similar work had been observed all round*, which has since been cleared away in removing the earth."

---

[1] Colonel Mackenzie's spelling of the name varied. It was sometimes "Amrawutty," sometimes "Amravutty," and sometimes, as in this map, "Amrawatty." Mr. Fergusson, in reproducing the map, very pardonably alters the spelling to the more, but still not quite, accurate "Amravati."

[2] Col. Mackenzie has marked 35 stones with yellow, saying, "The yellow colour denotes stones that are "entirely destroyed." From another section, not printed by Mr. Fergusson, it is clear that Mackenzie means stones destroyed but still *in situ*, their bases being seen. Mr. Fergusson's plan, however, having most of the inner circle, and a portion of the outer coloured yellow, prevents those individual stones from being recognised.

PLATE I.

(Description of this Plan, given above it, by Colonel Mackenzie,)

"Sketch of Deepauldinna
at AMRAWUTTY
in its present state,
March 1816."

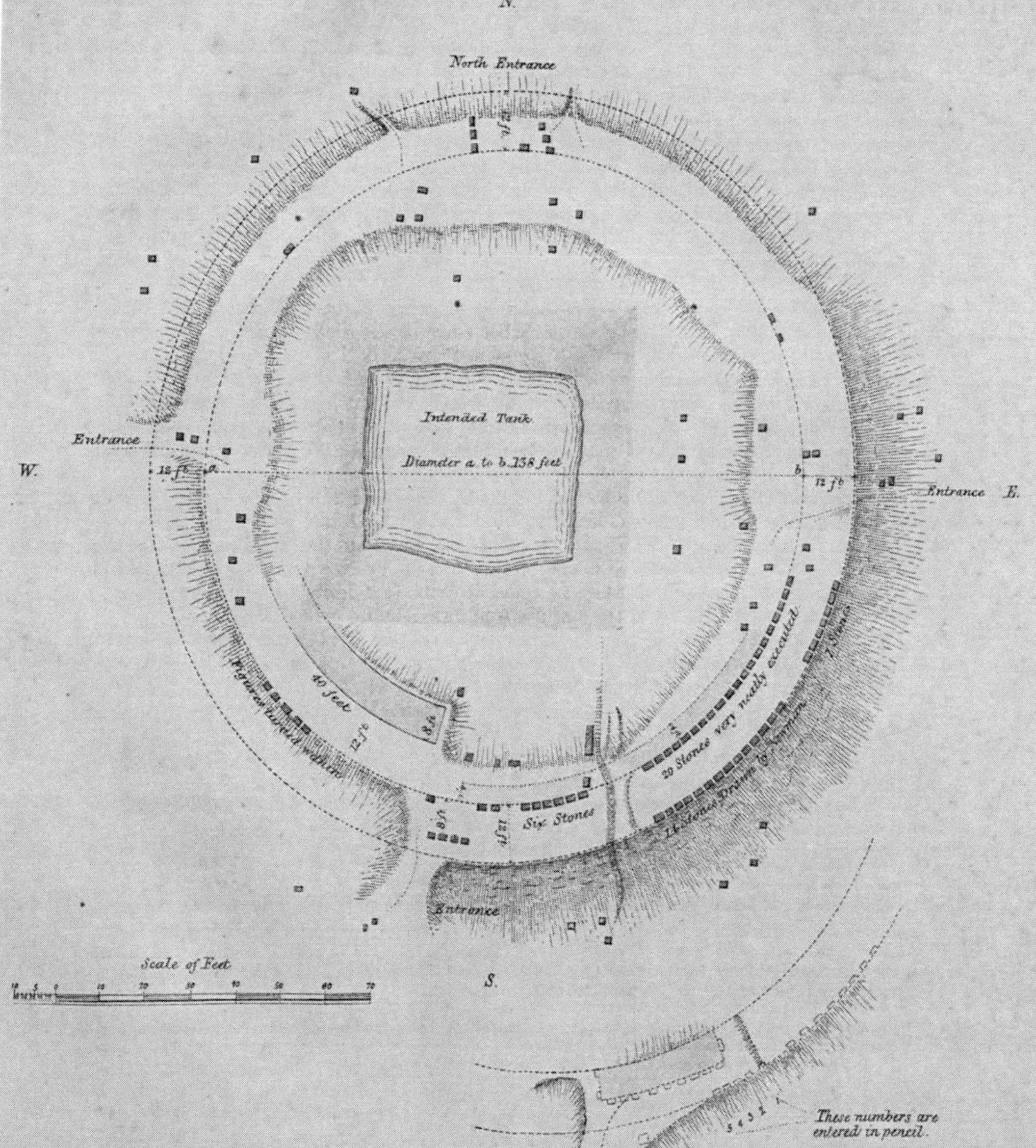

Colonel Mackenzie gives us the length and breadth of this "strong work," viz., 8 feet thick, he himself having seen 40 feet of it, and though the height is not specified he calls it a "wall."

The diameter of the inner circle of rail is 165 feet; and as this strong masonry circlet was 12 feet inside of this, its own outside diameter would be 141 feet, and the inside 125 feet, allowing 8 feet as its breadth.

I venture to submit that the existence of this circle of solid masonry destroys the basis for Mr. Fergusson's opinion that the space inside the double rail contained several detached buildings, a 30 feet circular marble Dâgoba, and a nine-storeyed Pagoda, a Vihára, a chaitya hall, a Dharmáśálá, and other conventual buildings all in wood (F., p. 182).[1] On the other hand, supposing this "*dinne*"—this "mound of lights"—to have been been really a mound, and therefore called by the Telugu natives by the proper term to describe it, we should expect it to have been a domed Tope such as that at Sánchi, and such as several others, also called "mounds" by the natives, in the immediate neighbourhood of Amarávati, where their remains still exist.[2]

This solid masonry 8-foot wall would then represent the lower position of the circular basement surrounding the dome, probably about 20 or 21 feet in height. The top of this wall would form the procession path or part of it. The diameter of the mound at the spring of the dome would be at the most 125 feet.

But it may be asked whether there are other reasons, besides the existence of the solid masonry wall and the Telugu appellation, for supposing the structure to have been a domed Tope. I reply by another quotation from Colonel Mackenzie himself. He has been describing the procedure of the Rajah Váśireddi Venkatádiri Naidu, of Chintapalli, who had destroyed the Tope 23 years before Colonel Mackenzie penned the description, but only one year before that gentleman first visited the spot (1797, the destruction having taken place in 1796). He states that the Rajah was obtaining valuable bricks by digging the mounds in the neighbourhood, where such bricks had been found, for the purpose of building the new town of Amarávati. The site of the Tope was then, apparently, simply a circular hill of earth with nothing to show the treasures it contained, for the workmen dug up two hillocks near (possibly the remains of minor domes) before they ever thought of searching at the Dípál-dinne. But the Mussulmen happening to dig into this mound discovered bricks, and also some sculptures which set the Rajah's mouth watering. He "eagerly came over to inspect

---

[1] Mr. Fergusson writes in a note, "So convinced am I of the correctness of this view that I had prepared "a drawing purporting to be a bird's-eye view of the Tope, with all these arrangements, and intended it should "form the frontispiece to this work. On second thoughts I abandoned the idea. All the other plates in the "work are absolute facts; this would have been said to have involved theories."

[2] On p. 176 (note [1]) of "Tree and Serpent Worship" Mr. Fergusson writes:—"*Dinne* means Sandbank in Telugu. This may be the origin of the name Dipal-dinne, which certainly does not mean 'Hill of lights.'" Having resided for nearly 10 years amongst a Telugu population, I may perhaps be permitted an opinion on this matter. As to the first word, "*dîpâl*," there can be no two opinions, "*dipâlu*" invariably signifying "Lights," "lamps," or "candles," the final *u* being elided by custom when such a word is affixed to another. "*Dinne*," it is true, means a "sand-bank," but it has a special signification which must not be lost sight of. Along the coast-line of the Krishṇâ Delta loose sand prevails, not only on the beach but often for a mile or two inland, and owing to the constant long-shore winds that blow with considerable force for a portion of every year, this sand is constantly being heaped and massed up against any obstruction. A group of palmyra trees with their long straight stems affords an excellent bulwark against the drifting sand, and wherever these are seen on such a coast, invariably there will be found heaped up, all round and amongst them, domes of sand frequently rising in a roughly circular form up to their very tops 60 or 70 feet above the ground level, with sides so steep that in many places it is impossible to mount them, and conspicuous for miles round. When riding down to the coast, on perfectly level country, these great white domes of sand with the branching palmyra tops sticking out of them form a most convenient landmark. As a further proof of how the sand drifts along that coast I may mention that a flourishing mercantile village, where deep sea prevails up to a very short distance of the shore, and where consequently there is excellent anchorage for coasting craft, has been so completely buried in sand that at the present day the ground level round the little custom-house is somewhat higher than the roof of the building! A casuarina plantation has been laid down to form a bulwark to the sand drift and protect the village. Now it is especially to these lofty domes of drifted white sand that the natives apply the name "*dinne*," or "sand-heap." And the term would be just such as the country people would apply to a lofty circular dome (perhaps coated with white plaster?) having at the top a great wooden umbrella, sticking out of it as the branching palmyra-tops stick out of the sand-hills on the coast. Possibly, as at Bharhut, the dome at Amarávati was illuminated on festival days. Hence the excellently descriptive title, "*Dipál-dinne.*"

"the place, and perceiving that it was the most curious of the several mounds he had "caused to be opened, conceived that it might embowel something of value; as most "places so marked are generally the receptacles of hidden treasures, he commanded the "Mussulmen to move elsewhere, as he designed to form a garden there, and a reservoir "in the centre." It is noteworthy that the Mussulman labourers were actually living on the slopes of this circular mound, ignorant of the treasures below. The Rajah then commenced to dig into the Dípál-dinne, "*the upper part of which rose in a turreted shape "to the height of* 20 *feet, which was cased round with bricks of unusual dimensions; the "diameter at top measured* 30 *yards.*"

A note describes the length of the bricks as 20 inches, "10 in breadth, and 4 thick."

This is confirmed by the earlier notes (*see above*). The "Memorandum" of 1803 says "to the southward of the village, close to it, is *a circular mound of about* 90 *feet in diameter, which had been cased round with bricks of a large size,* and slabs of white stone, sculptured so far as I could perceive by their remains there," etc. . . . . .

And the paper of 1807 says "*I conjecture that the whole had, previous to its opening, formed a solid circular mound.*"

Here we have an exact description of the ruined remains of an old Tope, such as are constantly met with in various parts of India, the remains of circular domes of the Sánchi type. As I have already stated, three others are to be seen in the neighbourhood of Amarávati, at Guḍiváḍa, at Bhaṭṭipról, and at Ghantaśála. I see no reason to doubt the accuracy of the information given to Colonel Mackenzie, as he was on the spot only a year after the Rájá's excavations, and those who described what had been there must have often seen the place and must have had its form fresh in their memory.

It was a circular mound sloping upwards from the level of the soil round about to the base of the central mass; which central mass, itself circular, rose in a turreted shape to the height of 20 feet, having a circular upper surface measuring 90 feet across, This turreted portion was "cased round" with large bricks, just as almost all the domed Topes are cased round. I have seen similar bricks from the Topes in the neighbourhood, and called attention to them in my previous paper on the antiquities of the neighbourhood of Bezwada. More than this, if the proportions of the Sánchi Tope are examined, and the estimates of "20 feet" and "30 yards" are not insisted upon as being absolutely accurate measurement by tape, it will be noticed that the width of the dome about 20 feet above the lower portion of it would bear to the base about the same proportion that 90 feet bears to a base of 125 feet in a structure of similar shape. It must be remembered that the lower portion must have been so concealed by the débris which had been at some former period thrown down from the summit of the dome that the true spring of the dome could not have been distinguished, and that Col. Mackenzie recorded only what he was told by the natives, so that we cannot reckon with absolute certainty on the measurements of 20 feet and 30 yards. But, taking them approximately, they represent exactly the remains of a ruined domed Tope of the Sánchi type.

The small plan is particularly valuable for another reason. At the south-east side of the circle inside the inner rail is a pink band 4 feet wide. For some time I was ignorant of what this was intended to represent, but Col. Mackenzie, in another portion of the paper quoted above, states "These inner slabs have been cemented to each other "with strong mortar, *and supported by a wall of masonry rising to a moderate height in "the rear.*" This is another feature apparently not noticed by Mr. Fergusson. It is impossible to say how high this wall was, or what it was used for, but it sufficiently accounts for the absence of carving on the back of the slabs belonging to the inner enclosure, and their remarkable thinness as compared with those of the outer. They were not intended to stand by themselves, but constituted the facing to a four foot circular wall of masonry.

All the above facts seem to me conclusive to prove that the real central structure at Amarávati was a circular domed Tope, probably having the Tee at its summit in marble, with a solid masonry ring round the base 8 ft. broad at the bottom, the diameter of the spring of the dome being 125 ft., and of the outer rim of the solid masonry wall at the base, 141 ft. Twelve feet from the foot of this wall all round ran a masonry wall 4 ft. thick faced with marble sculptures—the "Inner Rail." Thirteen feet outside this again was another ring of marble rail—the "Outer Rail,"—with four entrances, probably corresponding to those of the inner rail, and sculptured on both sides.

From the appearance of the south gateway in Mackenzie's large plan it would seem that a rail of seven pillars had been laid across the mouth of the inner rail at that point, so as to prevent the inner enclosure (between the inner rail and the dome) from being visible to eyes profane. And there is a hint of something similar at the west gateway, though the slabs would there appear to have been more disturbed. If this were the case, it would be reasonable to conclude that while the outer rail had four gateways, the inner had (subsequently) only one, three having been stopped up when the outer rail was erected.

The above arguments lead to the conclusion that Mr. Fergusson's theory, that the space within the inner rail was occupied by several detached buildings, is untenable. If there had been such, they would have been erected, partly in stone, partly in wood; and it would seem beyond the bounds of possibility that their ruined remains could assume the shape described by the natives to Colonel Mackenzie. Mr. Fergusson thinks the central structure of all to have been a marble-cased dagoba, 30 to 35 feet in diameter and 50 ft. high. But the central portion of the structure previous to the Rajah's excavations is described as a turreted mass of earth cased with large bricks 90 ft. in diameter at the top. The two things seem to me incompatible.

Moreover, I would call attention to the masses of earth that covered not only the central portion but the whole of the rails, so that the Rajah was ignorant of their existence, and a colony of Mussalman labourers was absolutely encamped on their slopes. Colonel Mackenzie states that "if the surrounding embankment was cleared, the inner "surface, where the stones are placed, would evidently appear to be on the same line of "level with the adjacent ground," and he is greatly puzzled to account for the presence of such masses of earth as covered the entire remains. He concludes that the whole heap of earth was brought from a distance, and deliberately heaped up over the sculptures for some purpose. And indeed such must have been the case if the interior of the rails was occupied by detached stone or wooden buildings, as supposed by Mr. Fergusson. For how else could the earth have got there? Certainly not by natural accumulation, as the site of the rails is the highest slope of ground about the town. Colonel Mackenzie further states that "immense quantities of broken bricks" filled the spaces between the two rows of stones. Mr. Fergusson thinks there was very little brick used in the construction of the central buildings. But even if there were—even if we grant that *all* the central buildings were composed of bricks, and that it was their utterly unrecognizable débris which covered the rails, how are we to account for the dome of earth cased round with immense bricks, and measuring 90 ft. across at the top, which occupied the centre of the circle, 20 ft. above the highest mass of earth accumulation round it?

I submit that all that we see from the plans and the descriptive letter-press forces to the conclusion that the Amarávati mound was one like that at Sánchi.[1]

The Rajah dug round the "eastern skirts of the high mound"—unfortunately it is not stated how far from the central mass, nor how deep, so that any deduction is impossible,—and there found "a small temple," near which was an image. Possibly this was at the site of the eastern gateway. It is certain, from my own observation and measurements, that the eastern gateway has been almost, if not quite, totally demolished. Two pillars were also found "a small distance west;" it is a pity the distances were not given, nor further particulars.

A "small building" and a copper lamp were also found at the western side of the mound; and at the lower portion of the mound on the north, apparently some distance outside the rail, was found a brick mandapam of four pillars and a headless image.

Extensive demolition on the north side followed, all the sculptured slabs being carried off to form a flight of twenty steps on the western side of the Śivagaṅga Tank beyond the town on the east. As before stated I was absolutely ignorant of the existence of this tank and never visited it. The slabs are possibly recoverable, and every effort should be made in this direction. They probably include a large portion of the northern section of the

[1] When I speak of a dome of the Sánchi type I mean simply a brick or earthen dome or tumulus as opposed to a stone building; not binding myself to the exact shape.

rails. Some other stones were carried off to the Śiva temple on the river bank, and some used "in various buildings, both public and private."

I have not seen any in private buildings, with the exception of a considerable number let in to the revetment of a deep and large-mouthed well or reservoir not far from the Tope to the west, whence they may possibly be recovered. (I removed three to Bezwada.) But there are a considerable number of slabs, many having the ends of sculptured figures on their surfaces still observable, on the towers and walls of the great temple of Amaréśvara (Śiva) on the river-bank. They were used as convenient slabs for binding together the masonry work of the buildings in progress, and were laid flat on the courses of brick already raised, and then built on; the workmen or their employers being utterly regardless of the beauty of the sculptures they bore. This is a great misfortune, for the Brahmans of the temple, and indeed of the whole country side, are bitterly bigoted;[1] and it is to be feared that Government may consider it unwise to sanction any interference with them. Persuasion, however, *may* result in permission being given for the removal of the marbles on condition of their places being replaced by other stones or masonry work. This has still to be tried. At present the Brahmans are passively hostile. The only real assistance I received was from the descendants of the Vásireḍḍi Rájá so often referred to, who still reside at Amarávati though greatly impoverished. By their aid I had two slabs removed from the inside to the outside of the temple wall, a course the priests of the temple were at first hotly opposed to.

Colonel Mackenzie's description of the treatment those marbles received which fell into the hands of the Mussulmans is amusing, though it is somewhat exasperating.

It will be observed that the Rajah never completed his work, and consequently many of the marbles are saved to us. He appears to have been at work, off and on, down to the year 1816, (for 20 years that is) till an inroad of Pindaries followed by his own death put a stop to all his designs.[2]

So much for the Rajah's labours. We now come to Colonel Mackenzie.

He had evidently intended to compile a folio volume full of his own descriptions, as well as the plans and drawings; for on a loose sheet, hastily scrawled in pencil in his own handwriting, is a sketch of the contents of the proposed volume; and the drawings and plans are so disposed in the volume before us as plainly to have been designed to illustrate the written matter which the other pages would have contained. The whole was to have been the first volume of a large and important undertaking, the title page being styled, "INDIA ANTIQUA ILLUSTRATA, *or an Essay to illustrate* THE ANCIENT "HISTORY, INSCRIPTIONS, AND RELIGIONS OF INDIA *by drawings of remarkable Sculptures,* "*Inscriptions, Buildings, Coins, and other existing remains of* ANTIQUITY." Unfortunately this was never carried out, and the pencil drafts of the contents is so badly written as to be almost illegible. Something, however, can be gained from the paper published by him in 1823, extracts of which have been given above, and from the notes here and there made on the plans and drawings.

It is necessary to observe that Col. Mackenzie has made an unaccountable mistake in the measurement of the diameter of the circle as given in his small plan. He calls it 138 feet, and scales it accordingly. But in his own description, as given above, we find him writing "The diameter of the inner circle measures 166 feet," and this we know to be nearer the real truth, from actual measurements as well as from his second enlarged plan.

Colonel Mackenzie gives a description of the position of the outer rail marbles *in situ*, which proves Mr. Fergusson's restoration of that part of the monument to be exactly correct.[3] But it is evident that in his time the upper portions of the pillars, as well as the architrave or coping stones, had been broken down, as he describes pillars

---

[1] They do not, as a rule, allow Europeans to cross even the threshold of the outer gates of their external Temple enclosures.

[2] The flooring of the platform round the deeper part of the tank was left altogether unfinished and irregular, as appears from the large Plan in F., XLVI., and especially the section given by Mackenzie and not printed by Mr. Fergusson.

[3] Except that Mackenzie does not mention or give a drawing of any portion of the animal frieze that Mr. Fergusson assigns to the base of this rail below platform level.

only six or seven feet high and having only two discs. The inner rail was, however, entire so far as it went. He describes the broad dagoba slabs flanked with small pillars "which are finished either with figures of lions and horses, or of men and women," and having the frieze "replete with figures" above.

The colouring on the sculptures which he describes would appear to have entirely disappeared, if indeed he were not mistaken altogether in thinking that the sculptures had been painted.

A great many slabs of a large size were seen by him lying about the surface of the sides of the tank which the Rajah had hollowed out, "but it is difficult to say where they "were originally placed." (*See the large Plan*, F., XLVII.) His description of these slabs clearly applies to such slabs as those given in F., XCIV., XCV., XCVI., and the localisation of these is one of the problems yet to be solved. I confess myself unable to give any opinion founded on facts; but if conjecture may be allowed a footing where there is nothing more substantial to put it out of court, I would suggest that possibly the 8-foot solid masonry wall forming the third and innermost concentric ring (which formed the base of the central dome?) may have been faced with marble sculptures. We know of the middle ring (the "inner enclosure" of the two rails) having been a masonry wall faced with marble sculptures, and it is not impossible that the innermost masonry wall was similarly faced.

It will no doubt be argued on the other hand that the basement member of all the sculptured dagobas represented in the marbles of the inner enclosure consists of the rail-ornament of pillars and discs, and that therefore, if the basement member of the central structure here were ornamented at all, we should expect to find it ornamented similarly with pillars and discs. This is true to a certain extent, but it must be observed that even at Sánchi, where the main structure was certainly a circular dome with a basement constituting a procession path, no such representation of a dome is to be seen in any one of the sculptures found there. The form of the dagoba universally carved, introduced as an object of reverence, is not that of the Sánchi dome, but something quite different. It does not therefore follow that because the sculptured dagobas have their basements ornamented with the rail design and certain other special features, therefore the basement members of domes of the Sánchi order had their faces similarly decorated. If therefore, as I believe, the central structure at Amarávati was like that at Sánchi, we are not bound to assume that the face of the masonry work surrounding the foot of the dome *must* have been decorated with marbles representing the rail-ornament. The facing marbles may possibly have been sculptured in some other fashion. For instance, the wall-facing given by Mr. Fergusson to the central dagoba, and depicted in his Plate No. XCIII., might possibly have been the facing to the basement member. Mr. Fergusson's elevation gives a wall of 21½ ft. high, and it is perhaps possible that the lower member of the Tope at Amarávati was of that height. The face of the corresponding wall at Sánchi was 17 ft. high, the base under all having a diameter of 121 ft. A base such as that at Amarávati of 141 ft. would give us proportionately a wall of nearly 20 ft. Possibly it was about 21½ ft. It must be noticed that all the slabs assigned to the central dagoba by Mr. Fergusson have the same quality of thinness as those of the inner enclosure, and that, like them, they were probably backed by masonry.

The differences between the positions of the stones in Mackenzie's plan of March 1816 and that of June 1817 is noticeable, but it is to be feared that little can be gathered to throw light on that point, as we have no consecutive account of work on which to go. But it is clear that some stones had been removed and sent down to Masulipatam.

We gather from the small plan that the Rajah had entirely removed the whole mass of earth and brick from the centre of the rails, and thrown it outside, but he had only cleared the outer rail on a portion of the southern and eastern section of the circle. The inner circle had almost all been dug up and removed, leaving standing only a series of stones in the south-eastern portion. Of the outer rail the section from the north-east round to the south had been exposed, and all except 21 stones had been removed. But the remainder were untouched, the earth covering them never having been removed. Little more excavation seems to have been carried on down to June 1817, only a portion of the space between the rails being thoroughly cleared and some further discoveries of marbles being made. The portion of the outer rail left untouched by the Rajah's workmen remained untouched by Colonel Mackenzie.

As to the tank in the middle, Colonel Mackenzie's section (*see* F., XLVII.) shows that its sides were perpendicular. If so it would seem to have been revetted, possibly with marbles, and search should be made for these. The tank is now very much filled up, only a hollow basin, in its lowest part seven feet below the level of the platform between the rails, being seen; and it is necessary that this should be excavated to the bottom of the Rajah's tank, in order to the recovery of the marbles used in its construction.

Annexed to the small plan is a small sketch showing the position of a few marbles about the south gateway. It will be seen that, in the process of clearing, the earth at the south part of the mound to the east of the entrance was cut into, and the outer rail opened up for a few yards distance. This resulted in the discovery of ten more marbles not previously recorded.[1]

The large plan shows us the state in which Colonel Mackenzie left the Tope in June 1817. From the extracts given above it would appear that more marbles were removed to the coast in later years. But we have no recorded account of further excavations having taken place till Sir Walter Elliot, in 1840, dug into "the northern "side of the west gateway, where a mound of earth concealed the modern chapel, "the walls of which furnished nine-tenths of the slabs now in the India Museum" (F., 182). But Sir Walter has never given a detailed account of his explorations, and we do not know in what state he found the Tope, nor in what state he left it.

It must be presumed that in course of years the rains washed back into the central tank the earth which had been thrown outside, and that gradually the same agency covered the platform and the marbles still lying on it with a thick coating of mud and débris; for when I visited the locality first in 1875 nothing was to be seen beyond a circular cup-like hollow, surrounded with irregular mounds of earth, and here and there marbles, considerably damaged, lying loosely about, or cropping up where the mounds were of less height. I shall revert to this more fully presently when describing my own operations. Meanwhile I pass on to an examination of the Mackenzie Drawings as compared with the marbles now in England.

[1] At east I take that to be the reason for the sketch having been made, unless it was simply a correction of the other, which is possible.

§ D.—THE MACKENZIE DRAWINGS AND THE SLABS NOW IN ENGLAND.

The Outer Rail.

MACKENZIE gives us drawings of the outer faces of four pillars, and the inner faces of ten, of the outer rail; and careful examination of his measurements and the shape of the stones shows us that, with one doubtful exception, these pillars are all separate ones, the drawings of the external faces in four instances not fitting the slabs whose internal faces are given. The doubtful exception is his No. 70, which represents the inner face of a pillar, of which his No. 56 *may* be the outer face. If this be the case, the volume gives us drawings of 13—if it be not the case of 14—pillars of the outer rail. But his Plan, the large one published by Mr. Fergusson, gives 21 such pillars *in situ.*

Of the discs, Mackenzie gives us five distinct pairs, (representing the middle and lower discs in each case,) two of the middle discs with spaces left on the page for the lower ones (these being in pairs in all probability), two middle discs separately drawn, and one lower disc separately drawn. This may be taken, then, as 10 groups of discs between pillars, the other discs of the same groups not being drawn. But the plan shows 19 groups, or spaces between pillars, occupied by at least one disc in position.

Of the coping, Mackenzie gives us three fragments only, one of the outer face and two of the inner, the stones being separate ones. This was to be expected, since the pillars are all broken off short, and the upper discs are missing in all cases. The coping stones of course had fallen, and in all probability had been carried off for the temple works, the labourers leaving in position those slabs which, being imbedded in the earth, were difficult to move. And the pillars so left of course held the intermediate discs, for it is impossible to move the discs without shifting the pillars to one side. The fact of the entire top of the outer rail on the south and south-east being broken off horizontally at about half its height enables us almost conclusively to presume that the force which broke that structure was a mass of earth or brick uniformly pressing with great power against the face of the rail. For if the destruction had been intentionally caused by direct human agency, the pillars would have been bodily removed, such a course being much easier than forcibly to fracture the entire upper portion of the rails.

The remaining member of the outer rail (pillars, discs, and coping having been mentioned) is the animal-frieze which Mr. Fergusson assigns to the base of the external face of the rail below platform level. It is remarkable that no single drawing is given by Mackenzie of any such sculpture. And it is reasonable to conclude from this fact that he saw none. Possibly these were excavated by Sir Walter Elliot. Two or three slabs belonging to that frieze were found during my own excavations lying about amongst the earth on the north-west, but I cannot state whether any others may remain still in position. I shall consider this question more fully hereafter.

Only one out of the three coping-stone slabs is now in England [1] (F., LXV. 2). It is impossible to say where it was found.

Of the 14 pillars, only one is in England. It is represented in F., LI. (left hand slab). Mackenzie has noted on the drawing (No. 31), "Exterior circle counting from the north, No. 1," and the paper bears also, above the pencil paging "50," the figure "No. 1," although another pencil mark is "A. 6." But it happens that a section line not given by Mr. Fergusson runs through the plan, and cuts across the northernmost stone on the east side of the exterior circle; and, the pillar being represented in the section, its measurement corresponds with the measurement given in the drawing and with the

[1] Mr. Fergusson has photographed all the Amarávati marbles now in the British Museum.

photograph given by Mr. Fergusson. I take it, therefore, as certain that the pillar shown in F., LI., was the northernmost slab on the east side of the outer rail.

Of the discs, again, drawn by Mackenzie's assistants, only one—that represented in F., LXII. (upper photograph)—is in England. Mackenzie notes this as "the best finished sculpture in Depaldinna," but beyond "outer circle," does not localise it.

Thus, of all the 32 pillars discs and coping stones drawn by Mackenzie and seen by him in position, only one piece of coping, one pillar, and one disc are in England. *Where are all the rest?*

The Inner Rail.

Of 24 Inner Rail Dagobas, drawn by Mackenzie, only six are in England. These are the slabs photographed in F., LXXVI., the upper and the lower right hand slabs in LXXVIII., the upper one in LXXIX., the right hand lower one in LXXX., and the upper one in LXXXI. Eighteen Dagobas drawn by Mackenzie are not in England. I only know of one in India, at Masulipatam. *Where are the rest?*

Of the six in England, that given in F., LXXX. (right hand lower slab), and that in F., LXXXI. (upper photograph), have in the Mackenzie Drawings respectively, "Inner Circle, No. 1, to the North-east," and "Inner Circle, No. 2, to the North-east," written on them. The positions of the other four are undiscoverable.

Colonel Mackenzie marks on the north-east of the inner circle only two stones as in position—namely, the above two.

The positions of several others can be conjectured from his notes, but as they are not in England I pass them over.

Of the inner rail pillars which occupied the spaces between the dagobas, in groups of three, Colonel Mackenzie gives drawings of five middle pillars, and six side ones. Two of the middle pillars are in England, and are to be seen in Mr. Fergusson's elevation of the Inner Rail (Plate LXXV.), but there is nothing on Mackenzie's drawings to guide us as to their position. Two of the side pillars are also in London, and are given in Mr. Fergusson's elevation, but the rest are missing.

Four drawings are given, in the MS. volume, of pieces of the coping-frieze of the inner enclosure, none of which are in England.

The Central Structure.

Mackenzie gives drawings of eight fragments of the central structure as assigned by Mr. Fergusson. Of these four are in England. These are to be seen in F., XCV., 3 and 4, XCVI., 1, and the left upper photograph in XCVII. There is nothing to guide us as to the position of XCV., 4. But the drawing in Mackenzie corresponding to XCV., 3, is noted as a "loose stone lying on the East side;" XCVI., 1, is a "loose stone lying on the South side;" and the stone given in XCVII. is a "loose stone to the east."

Unassigned Fragments.

Seventeen drawings of unassignable fragments are to be seen in Mackenzie's volume, but only one, and that half broken, is in England. Mr. Fergusson photographs it in Plate XCVI., 3.

Here, then, we have given us by Colonel Mackenzie's assistants 97 carefully executed drawings of separate marbles, 132 being the number of marbles whose positions are recorded by him in the plan. But, of these 97, only 18 are in England. Where are the remaining 79? They are not at Bezwada, the marbles there being different. I know of only two at Masulipatam, an inner enclosure dagoba in splendid preservation, and an outer rail pillar (which may possibly be two of those preserved to memory in Mackenzie's drawings. Further examination is necessary). There are two outer rail pillars at Madras, which also want examination. Mackenzie records that 11 stones were sent to Calcutta. At the best, then, we can account for 15. *Where are the remaining 64?*

PLATE II.

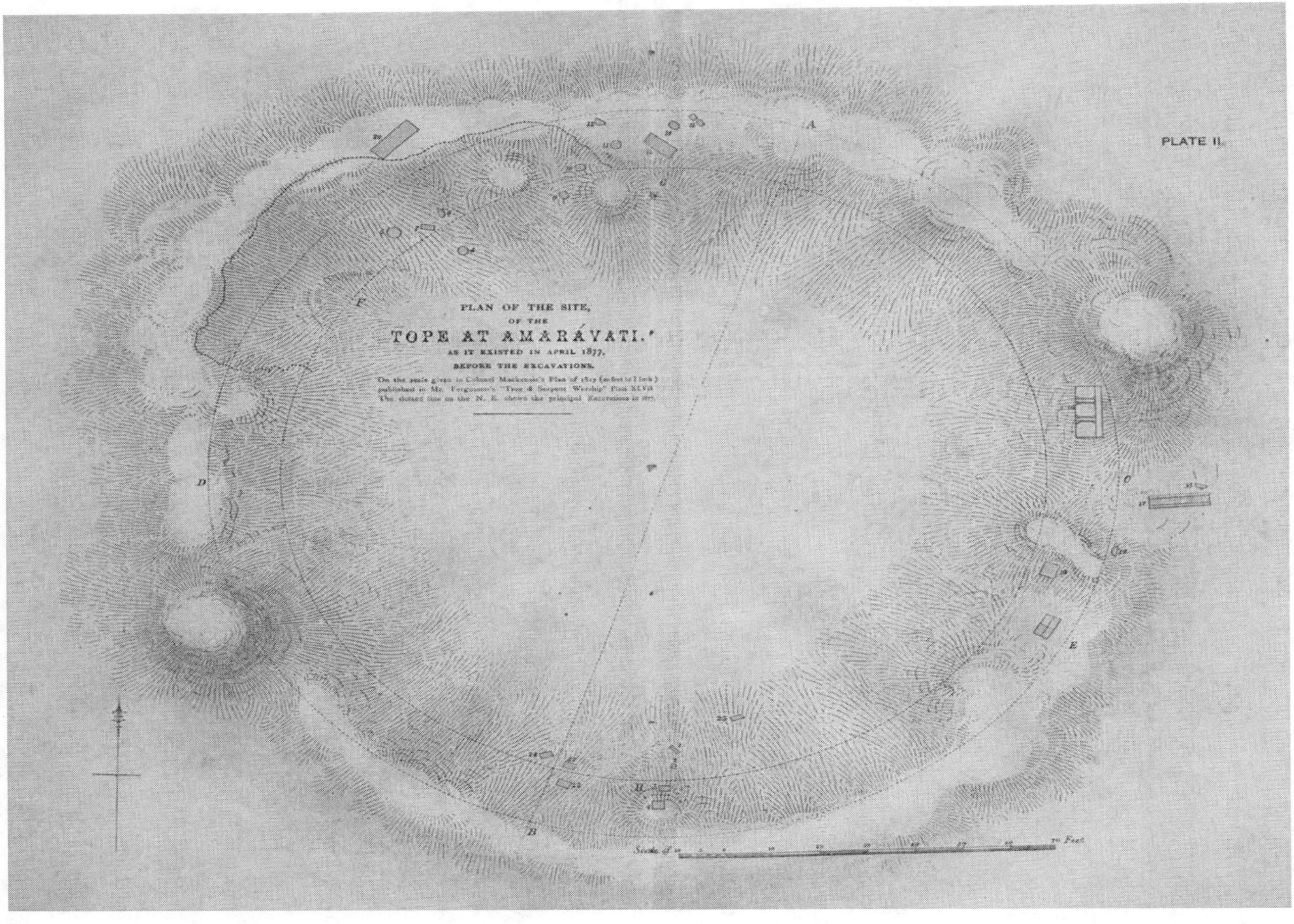

PLAN OF THE SITE,
OF THE
TOPE AT AMARÁVATI.
AS IT EXISTED IN APRIL 1877,
BEFORE THE EXCAVATIONS.
On the scale given in Colonel Mackenzie's Plan of 1817 (20 feet to 1 inch)
published in Mr. Fergusson's "Tree & Serpent Worship" Plate XLVII
The dotted line on the N. E. shows the principal Excavations in 1877.
A
B
C
D
E
F
Scale of
Feet

§ E.—EXCAVATIONS IN 1877.

I now come to my own connection with the Tope at Amarávati. I joined the District in January 1875, but till September of that year had no opportunity of visiting it. In that month, finding myself at one of our taluq stations a few miles up stream, I determined to visit Amarávati and see the monument personally. A couple of hours sail brought me abreast of the old fort of Dharaṇikóṭa, where I landed and was taken to the *Dîpâldinne*.

I found there no trace whatever of the Chintapalli Rajah's reservoir, except a hollow cup-like basin surrounded by a mound of earth and stones, sloping much more steeply on the inside than the out. This circular mound varied from 150 to 200 feet across, the earth being irregularly displaced, mounds of ordinary size alternating with much higher ones, and the whole being intersected with channels down which watercourses had been hollowed by many successive rainy seasons. On the supposition that the rail had four gateways on the cardinal points, the highest mounds were just south of the west gateway and just north of the east gateway, where the surface of each was 24 feet above the centre of the circle.

A few somewhat damaged and discoloured marbles were lying here and there, and a fine but terribly mutilated slab (No. 20 of my list) was fully exposed on the top of the mound on the west. It had been unearthed for exhibition to the Collector of the District and being left uncovered was speedily mutilated by the shepherd boys of the village, who broke off all the exquisitely sculptured and delicate faces and limbs of the figures—a fate which will inevitably overtake every marble left unguarded at the village. It is impossible for the village officials to prevent this destruction, for their duties prevent their being always on the slopes of the ruined Tope. All marbles uncovered must be removed to a museum, or specially guarded by paid watchers.

I had a slight excavation made in the low mound on the south, and found two small marbles (Nos. 1 and 2 of my List) imbedded near the surface. I then had all the exposed stones covered with earth, and left the place: not feeling myself at liberty to explore further without authority.

From the month of June 1876, when that authority was received, I was constantly trying to find time to visit Amarávati; but my ordinary official work perpetually stood in the way, and till the end of April 1877 I was unable to commence operations.

Then I set to work. My first care, after measuring the width of the basin in a few places, was to fix the cardinal points as accurately as possible, and prepare a rough working plan on which to record the positions of the marbles. This is given in Plate II. of this Paper. It is prepared exactly on Colonel Mackenzie's lines. My circles correspond with his, and I have added his line of section A, B as a guide. My cardinal points are C, D, G, H. E. is the locality where I first discovered what I erroneously thought was the platform. F. the spot where the real platform was unearthed and the principal excavations conducted.

At E, where I commenced work, I had seen at my former visit four marbles lying flat, with smooth surfaces, and arranged so evenly side by side as evidently to have been placed there as a floor or platform. They were 7 feet above the level of the centre of the basin, and were imbedded in the surrounding mound at a place where it is about 15 feet high. I uncovered these and examined them. They were all very evenly smoothed and squared, but bore no sculpture. Replacing them I went to the south of the circle at H, and found the two stones I had excavated on the previous occasion. They were lying almost at the lowest level, the rains of 1875 and 1876 having washed them down and formed a watercourse there. These I numbered 1 and 2.

§ F. DETAILED DESCRIPTION OF MARBLES EXCAVATED IN 1877, AND OTHERS IN INDIA.

I PURPOSE to give as close a description as I can of each separate marble, and in doing so shall adhere to Mr. Fergusson's nomenclature, such as "outer rail," "inner enclosure," "pillars," "discs," and the like, so that I may readily be understood by all acquainted with or possessing Mr. Fergusson's work. My descriptions, as already stated, are written up from notes and measurements taken on the spot, in some cases assisted by rough photographs taken by an unskilled native artist at the time. It is to be hoped that the Government will have them all carefully photographed, if the originals are not soon transmitted to this country. I tried my best to have all the photographs taken to scale, so as to render them better able to be compared with the pictures already published, but I cannot guarantee the scientific accuracy of the scale, because we had no appliances at hand to guide us except a roughly marked tape which was laid on the object-glass of the camera every time a photograph was taken. The measurements I give, however, of each marble will enable those interested in the subject to correct errors of the photographs where these may be inaccurately scaled. The scale adopted is Mr. Fergusson's—1 inch to 1 foot.

No. 1. (2 ft. 6 in. by 1 ft. 3 in.) End of the roll-ornament which constituted the main design of the frieze forming the coping of the outer rail. As in No. 4, Plate XCII. (F.), this fragment shows a fish-monster swallowing the end of the roll. It is broken at the top and bottom, and the back is split off. The piece is much weatherworn. Compare my No. 78 where the end of the roll is swallowed in a very comical fashion by a *gaṇa*, or dwarf.

It is necessary to note that these few marbles, being excavated at the due south point of the circle, belong in all probability to the parts of the monument about the south gateway. This fragment would therefore naturally be expected to be found here, the roll-frieze having an end just where the sculptures about the gateway begin.

It is worthy of interest, too, to observe that the fish-monster's head swallowing the roll is copied into early Brahmanical sculptures about the Krishṇá River; as at Uṇḍavilli in the rock-cut temple there, and various other places in the neighbourhood. Sometimes it is used as a subordinate ornament decorating folds of the roll itself, as in F., LVI. 1.

No. 2. (1 ft. 7 in. by 1 ft.) A fragment of one of the outer rail pillars. (F., L. to LIII.) This has a portion of a lotus-disc, and of a fold of leaf-like ornament above. It is much broken and weatherworn. The back is broken off.

A slight excavation just above where these stones were lying brought to light a small stone (No. 3) smoothly squared and laid flat so as to form a step or flooring. This being at the same level as the four paving stones near E. induced me to think that they were all parts of the platform. But as the excavation proceeded another stone (No. 4) appeared at a level 3 ft. 10 in. higher up the bank, also laid flat, and unsculptured in any way.

No. 3. (1 ft. 8 in. by 10 in.) Flat paving stone, unsculptured.

No. 4. (2 ft. 10 in.) square—similar. This was lying flat, and on its upper surface appeared the remains of some broken brick-and-plaster work. The stone was only six inches below the surface level of the bank at that spot, and was 10 ft. 10 in. above the level of the centre of the hollow basin.

As the explorations proceeded, and it became known that I was going to employ labourers, numbers of coolies and women began to flock to the mounds. I therefore determined to examine and note the positions of the remainder of the exposed marbles before I dug any further, and then to set different gangs to work systematically at the digging. The exposed stones would in any case have to be removed, and it seemed desirable to do this before proceeding further. Several stones were lying on the surface of the bank at the north and north-west side of the circle, and others were partially appearing above the ground at different levels. These I shall now describe.

No. 5 was the most westerly of these exposed stones and was lying on the surface. It is one of the discs of the Outer Rail, having the lotus design on both sides. Diam. 2 ft. 7 in., including the external flower-ornament band. The lotus design alone 2 ft. 1 in. The flanges that supported it in the holes in the sides of the pillars are broken. The marble in the British Museum that most closely approximates to it in size is the right hand upper disc figured in F., Pl. LV.

It is to be observed that these discs, though similar in design, are often found to vary in size, and that a similar variation is found with the uprights, some being 18 inches shorter than others. Was this due to studied negligence? or actual carelessness, different marbles being sculptured by different artists? Or to the fact that the rails were not all executed at one time, as seems clearly shown by the style of the marbles and the characters of the inscriptions they wear? Or were different parts of the rail deliberately made of differing heights? From the marbles unearthed by me little can be learned in this respect.

These questions may be determined after careful examination of all the remains, and the record of measurements and the position in which the marbles may be found lying, but it would be premature to theorize till the entire remains have been unearthed.

In a watercourse close by No. 5, and at a low level, evidently washed down, was lying another disc, No. 6.

No. 6. Lotus disc of Outer Rail having the flanges broken off. It has the lotus ornament on both back and front. On one side the sculpture is well preserved, but on the other it is much weatherworn. Including the flower band round the design the diameter of the disc is 2 ft. 10 in., without it 2 ft. 4 in. It corresponds with the lower left-hand disc in F., Pl. LV.

Partly visible higher up on the bank, and only 4 ft. below the level of the highest part of the mound at that place, was a stone which I uncovered, and numbered 7.

No. 7. (3 ft. 4 in. by 1 ft. 7 in.). Base of one of the pillars of the Outer Rail, broken top and bottom. It corresponds to the pillars of the smaller and plainer class seen in F., Pl. LIII. The lower half disc, with one of the lotus-buds at the side, and the plain treble-fluted shafts are to be seen. On each side are to be seen the mortice holes into which fitted the flanges of the discs of the rail.

This piece was entirely out of position. Near it was a quantity of broken brick and plaster, and close by this, at the subsequent excavations, I found a large mass of the same material lying on the platform level. It was however quite shapeless, and it is impossible to say to what it belonged. Till all the marbles are unearthed it would be useless to speculate, but I may point to stone No. 4 as showing that brick and plaster was apparently used on a marble laid as foundation; and along the front of Nos. 26, 27, 28 (pillars and disc *in situ*) runs a line of plaster 1 ft. 10 in. above the platform level, as if some later work had been carried on destroying the existing sculptures. Taken by themselves these instances would tend to show that brick and plaster was a material used at a later date when the sculptures were unappreciated, and did not form part of the original design.

Close to No. 7 the edge of another marble showed itself above the ground, and I dug this up, giving it the next consecutive number. It is the base of one of the pillars of the Outer Rail, and was lying on its side in a slanting position.

No. 8. Sculptured on one side only, with the back rough, or perhaps split off. Base of a pillar of the Outer Rail. It has the lower half disc and the disc above it complete. Between them the shaft is as usual divided into three slightly curved panels, but in this case these are plain and unornamented. (F., LIII. 1.)

Further to the east at about 25 or 30 feet distance, and close to the inner edge of the mound, almost at its highest level, was another stone, of which a fragment showed itself above ground. This was No. 9.

No. 9. (2 ft. 8 in. by 2 ft.) Right hand lower half of one of those curious vases or bowl-like figures which Mr. Fergusson places at the base of the centre dagoba. (See the lowest fragment on the left of Plate XCIII., and Plate XCVI. 4. This is in all respects similar.) Back broken off, or never smoothed. (*Photographed.*)

These vases appear to represent some large earthenware vessels, out of which grow a number of lotuses and other flowers. They were evidently placed at the base of some panelled wall, for the dividing rib is seen in each case. The vases were decorated richly with wreaths similar to those seen on the dagobas represented in these sculptures. The base is covered with an elegant and flowing design, possibly intended to represent water.

Are they funeral urns? The gay wreaths thrown round them, and the decorations giving them apparently honours similar to those bestowed on the dagobas, would perhaps justify this theory. If so, the flowers bursting from them might symbolize the after-life.

Mr. Fergusson places these at the base of a wall, and it is to be observed as confirmatory of his view that similar designs are to be seen at the base of the central panel in all the dagobas represented in the sculptures already found. The figure is also used at the base of sculptured pillars and panels in other Buddhist buildings, where the main ornament running up the side is designed of twisted and intertwined flowers (compare Fergusson's "*Indian and Eastern Architecture,*" woodcut 100, stelæ at the end of the stairs, Abhayagiri Dagoba). I have also seen them at the base of jambs of doorways in many Hindu temples in the neighbourhood, as well as on the rock-cut temple at Uṇḍavilli.

The next two marbles were found lying on the surface a few feet from No. 9. They were close by where the north gateway must have stood if there was one; but as the bank at this point is not very high it is probable that the structure has been greatly demolished.

No. 10. (3 ft. by 3 ft.) Base of one of the pillars of the Outer Rail. Only one face remains, showing part of the lower frieze of flowers. The other face is broken or cut off so evenly that I think it probable that the marble was used for a portion of the paving of the stonework of the Rajah's tank.

No. 11. One of the Outer Rail discs, having the lotus ornament on both sides. (Diameter, with the external flower-band, 2 feet 10 inches; without it, 2 feet 4 inches.) This is a pair to No. 6.

While engaged at this work the labourers occupied in screening earth at the south of the circle brought me an iron implement found in the earth close by No. 3. It is in shape something like a hoe, very much rusted and injured.

Close by No. 11 on the surface was lying No. 12.

No. 12. (2 ft. 1 in. by 1 ft. 3 in.) Half of an Outer Rail disc. It is very much weatherworn, and the back is broken, or has been cut off. Unimportant.

I may mention here that the "Pâlnâd marble" of which these stones are made seems to split in blocks easily, and many of the marbles seem to have been broken lengthwise. This may be due to accident, but it is possible that this quality may have led to their being purposely split.

Almost exactly at the north point, lying exposed in part, was a fine slab evidently part of the Outer Rail coping. I dug up the whole of this, and was well rewarded by finding a large and very interesting piece, though unfortunately much weatherworn.

No. 13. (7 ft. 3 in. by 2 ft. 8 in.) Portion of the Outer Rail coping. On the outer side is the roll-ornament. On the inner is a very spirited and animated battle scene. This is especially interesting, because so few battle scenes are depicted on these sculptures. I can only find two amongst those now in England. One is found in F., LXI. 1, but even that does not represent any fighting. The only really fighting scene is that on the central right hand upper panel of the dagoba in F., Plate LXXVI., and Mr. Fergusson thinks that the subject "ought not to appear on a Buddhist monument." No. 13 is also interesting because there is on it a representation of two chiefs in chariots, Mr. Fergusson having especially noted (p. 196) that chariots were conspicuous by their absence at Amarávati, though "so prominent at Sánchi." It is a great pity that this slab is so much injured. The whole of the left portion is gone, and the right is much damaged

It represents the hurried flight of a beaten prince within his castle walls, closely pressed by the enemy, with whom a running combat is kept up. The defeated chief standing up in his chariot engages with the bow the chief of the pursuing army, who in his turn is represented as standing in a chariot and armed with a bow. The horses of both chariots are being urged along at full galop by their drivers. Below the first-mentioned chariot two horsemen meet one another in full charge. They appear to be armed with swords. Below the horsemen again, in the foreground, is a combat of foot soldiers with short swords, and close by their side the horse of one of the pursuers stumbles and falls. This horse is admirably rendered. He has been going at speed, and his fall is complete. The head is doubled under the fore legs, which are stretched in front of him but bent at the knee joint. The hind legs still support the weight of the body, but with a powerful muscular effort that shows how momentary the attitude is; another instant and they too will succumb. The rider has managed things very well, and in spite of the evident violence of the accident maintains his balance in the saddle. Behind this horse in the thick of the fighting are two foot soldiers. One has seized the other by the throat, and with excited action threatens his life. The defeated soldier, who has been disarmed, calmly disdainful of death stands in a firm and dignified attitude awaiting his fate, both hands resting on the hips. Below them lies a dead body. Above, one of the pursued falls back wounded or killed with his hand clasping his head. The whole of this group of struggling soldiery is strikingly natural and highly animated. In the right hand corner the horse of one of the pursuers is seized round the neck and strangled by an elephant belonging to the beaten army. The horse is falling. The rider grasps the elephant's tusks as if in a vain attempt to disengage the grip. (This stone bears an inscription.)

Now comes the question as to the subject of this sculpture. In the case of the Bharhut Tope there are no battle scenes or sieges of any kind depicted in the sculptures, and there is only one soldier standing easily as if on guard. The sculptures at Buddha-Gaya bear no trace of military life, still less of warfare. I have searched through General Cunningham's and Mr. Burgess's Reports in vain to find any battle scenes on Buddhist sculptures elsewhere than at Sánchi. If there had been such a scene at Bharhut we might have discovered a clue to the subject, as almost all the groups there have been inscribed with a note showing the story they represent. But there is nothing of the kind. Turning for information to the volumes published containing the Buddhist legends and "Játakas," I find in the whole of the "*Abhinishkramana Sutra*" (Beal's "*Romantic History of Buddha*") no allusion to any scene of fighting whatever. In Hardy's "*Manual of Buddhism*" I can only find three allusions to any actual fighting. One is the war between the *Nága* kings *Chulōdana* and *Mahōdana* in Ceylon, to stop which Buddha made his second journey to Ceylon. This does not seem to apply to the group under discussion, as the combatants are said in the story to have been veritable *nágas* (p. 208). The second is where the herculean warrior Bandhula slaughters the 500 princes of Lichawi with one arrow from his bow (p. 282). But this cannot be the subject of the marble in question. The third is, I think, the most probable, and I give the account *in extenso*. (Hardy, p. 285).

"The monarch now reigning at Kosol was Pasé-Nadi, the son of Maha Kósala, whose " daughter had been given in marriage to Bimsara king of Rájagaha. As her portion " she received the city of Sewet, which was situated on the border of each kingdom; " but when her son, Ajásat, killed his father, Pasé-nadi took back the city by force. A " war ensued, as Ajásat was resolved to retain it; at one time the victory inclined to the " side of Kosol, and at another to Rájagaha. At last Ajásat, to decide the contest, took " his sword and shield, and rushed into the midst of his opponent's army, where he slew " great numbers so that the king of Kosol was obliged to retreat. Upon a swift horse " he fled and approached the city . . . . ." This story occurs in the *Játaka* of the flower girl who, because she made an offering to Buddha, became the wife of this beaten king of Kosala, and was called *Kosála-Malliká-Déví*.

Even at Sánchi there appears to be only one scene of warfare on the sculptures, namely that depicted in F., Pl. XXXVIII., and that is apparently a siege, where the only actual fighting takes place close under the walls, other parts of the field being occupied by seemingly peaceful processions.

I regret to say that my (very amateur) native photographer took only three copies from the negative in the case of this marble. One is in the hands of the Madras Government. One was sent to General Cunningham. One I gave to Mr. Fergusson.

Close to No. 13 was lying No. 14 fully exposed, and seriously injured on the upper surface, as well as much weatherworn.

No. 14. Disc of the Outer Rail, of exactly the same dimensions as No. 6, and having the lotus or waterleaf ornament on both sides.

With reference to these discs, repeated so constantly, with such infinite fanciful variety of detail but so similar in their design, there can be little doubt that the ruling idea is an imitation of the full-blown lotus flower. Mr. Fergusson calls them "circular "discs covered with a lotus or waterleaf ornament." (F., p. 92.) On the pillars of most of the rails of the class the four angle-corners requisite to be filled in order to give horizontal lines across the marble above and below the circular disc, are occupied by half-blown lotus-buds. The circular "waterleaf" design probably represents the full-blown flower. In no other way can the irregularly placed little circles on the central boss be accounted for than by the supposition that they represent the ends of the petals as seen when the flower is fully open and held facing the observer. Notice the conventional way of treating the full-blown flower in all these sculptures. Take, for instance, the lotuses at the base of F., LXXII., fig. 2. It will be at once seen that the flower consists of a number of leaves enfolding the collected mass of petals, which mass is represented with a circular top, while the outer circlet of leaves is depicted falling back quite separate from the inner circlet. All the leaves have the shape that constitutes the characteristic form of the disc ornaments. Compare this with the inmost member, the *matrix* of any of the discs, and the resemblance will be found complete. The outer circles of the disc-ornamentation are, of course, merely conventional, and are treated in various ways. Mr. Fergusson thinks that the design originated in the fact that "when the rail was "in wood, nails with large heads or metal plates were used to keep the structure in form, "as is still sometimes done in framed doors or gateways, and that these afterwards "became ornaments, and were used architecturally, as we find it here and elsewhere." (F. 90. *n.* 5.)

Close to No. 14 were lying two small pieces of broken marble unsculptured, and unimportant. I numbered these 15. (*a* and *b*). They require no comment.

There being no more stones visible above the surface at the north side of the circle I went round to the east, where, just north of my east point, I saw a slab showing slightly above ground. I had this excavated, and it proved to be one of very large size and belonging to a class different from any yet discovered.

No. 16. It is a large slab in much plainer style than most of the others. (13 ft. long by 6 ft. high.) A plain surface divided by half-pilasters into three panels. At the bottom is a rough base 1 ft. 8 in. high, which apparently lay below ground. Underneath are two tenons to fit into holes in the foundation. Above this rough base the slab would form a wall 13 ft. long by 4 ft. 4 in. high. The left panel is 3 ft. wide, the middle one 3 ft. 10 in., the right hand one 3 ft. 10 in. The right hand end of the slab is gone. The design was evidently continued, and the slab when perfect must have been of great size and weight. Its back is blank. The panels are divided by small pilasters, ornamented at the base by figures of lions, elephants, and *gaṇas,* and at the capitals by winged lions.

At first sight it seemed probable that this slab formed part of the returns of the east gateway, but on comparing it with the gateways at Sánchi and Bharhut as given by Mr. Fergusson and General Cunningham, this theory plainly falls to the ground, the entire breadth of the *toraṇ* gateway measuring only some 7 or 8 feet. Supposing the edifice inside the rails to have been a domed tope as at Sánchi, Bharhut, and other places, it would be reasonable to look for the tee at its summit; and the dome being destroyed we might hope to find fragments of the tee amongst the marbles now left. But the erect lower portion of the tee at Sánchi would appear to have been only 11 ft. 6 in. square and 6 ft. high, whereas this slab was more than 13 ft. long. The sides of the tee-wall, too, were fashioned after the manner of the rails, whereas this was smoothed, flat, and divided into probably four panels by carved half-pillars. Nevertheless, if we may suppose the tee at Amarávati to have been about 14 ft. 6 in. square instead of 11 ft. 6 in., then this slab might have been one side of it; for the number of pilasters and panels here would correspond with the number of uprights and rail-stones on the Sánchi tee, and the lower portion (1 ft. 8 in.) might have been sunk in a pedestal. On the other hand this is pure supposition, and Mr. Fergusson does not think there was a tumulus and tee at all. If he is correct, this solid marble wall must have formed part of some building of which as yet we have no other trace.

Not far from this slab, and just on the south side of the highest mound on the east, close in fact to the site of the eastern gateway, is a piece of a fallen eight-sided pillar. It is not far from the northernmost of the two small circles on Colonel Mackenzie's plan, which appear to me probably to represent pillars external to the rail.

No. 17. Pillar of eight sides, having a two-line inscription in Páli, and a long inscription in apparently about 13th century Telugu characters. Two of the sides are broader than the others. Above the Páli inscription is a curious flourishy scroll, apparently consisting of letters, but which I am quite unable to decipher. On the base of the pillar is a roughly cut triple umbrella gracefully designed.

The Páli inscription simply declares that "Himala, son of the householder Vasu-"mitasa, with his wife, his son, his sister, and his daughter, made a gift of the pillar." As to the scroll, General Cunningham, to whom I sent a tracing, tells me that he has found similar ones on many of the pillars of the Buddhist era in the north—that he believes them to be some sort of writing—and that he does not despair some day of the clue to it being discovered. Being unwell at the time, I had no opportunity of studying the Telugu-Sanskrit inscription, but I sent an impress of it to the Madras Government Museum, along with some fifty other stone inscriptions of considerable importance in the neighbourhood, and some day I hope to have leisure to publish it. I am sanguine enough to hope that it may prove of importance. Meanwhile it lies in the Central Museum, Madras, and will probably not be touched.

Not far from this pillar, but on the inner edge of the circular mound, and near the squared floor-stones formerly mentioned as having been found near the point E. in my plan, I found another slab partly exposed. This I completely unearthed and afterwards had photographed.

No. 18. (2 ft. 6 in. square.) A portion of the Outer Rail coping. One side has the roll-ornament, with its supporting figure; the emblem resting above the fold of the roll being in this instance the dagoba. On the inner side is a fragment of sculpture. On the left is seen a palace balcony, in which sits a chief and his wife, attended. Below, as if in the courtyard, an elephant is apparently bending in salute of his master. From the castle gates there rides a prince on horseback, with two footmen and an elephant and horsemen in attendance. The prince is riding up to a gateway of the Sánchi type (which General Cunningham calls a "*toraṇ*" gate), but his way is barred by a person who holds up a warning hand to him. Just in the gate stands a man with an umbrella, but whether this sign of loyalty is to be referred to the horseman, or to the man who bars his progress, does not clearly appear. Inside the gate is a building of some kind (the marble breaks off here), at the doorway of which three persons are worshipping. The horsemen would not appear to be Siddhârtha, as there is no glory round his head or other distinguishing mark.

In a watercourse close above No. 18 I found No. 19 lying partly exposed.

No. 19. Disc of the outer Rail (diameter 2 ft. 6 in). It has the lotus ornament on both sides, and is well preserved. The flanges are broken off, only a portion of one remaining.

While engaged in excavating this stone I was informed that the workmen had finished cleaning the earth from a large marble lying on the bank at about the north-west point. This was the marble that I mentioned above as having been exposed to view by the villagers for a late Collector and having after his departure been greatly injured by idle boys. It had been covered with earth at my visit two years previously, and now was brought out for examination. I gave it the number 20, and had it photographed.

No. 20. (10 ft. 7 in. long by 2 ft. 9 in.) Portion of the Outer Rail coping-stone. The outer face as usual has the roll. Four folds are seen on this slab, and the emblems supported above the roll are two dagobas with their attendant worshippers, a pillar holding on the top three dwarfs in attitude of prayer, and the empty throne with the wheel of the law (or sun-emblem ?) above it, and its worshippers. Beneath each of these emblems, on the roll itself, is a square entablature. On one are seen two male and two female worshippers adoring the sacred tree, throne, and feet impressions. On another is an arabesque ornament. On a third four persons are worshipping an object that looks like an earthen pot placed on a pedestal. The fourth has two *makara-* (or fish-monsters'-) heads, swallowing the end of the roll, and divided by a straight band having three lotus discs. Compare the upper fragment in F., LVI. The roll has the usual supporters.

The inner face, as usual, has a sculptured scene. In the centre is seen the throne and feet impressions under a bo-tree, which overshadows a canopy erected above them. Under the canopy are two worshippers. On the left side of this is a litter, containing two persons, which is being lifted into the air by *gaṇas*. In front of the litter a horse bounds into the air with a bold spring, very ably rendered. Below these are a number of attendant *gaṇas*, one of whom is in the act of mounting a horse. Another horse is represented as in full trot. Underneath, an empty litter lies on the ground. The litter mounting into the air comes from a castle gate. On the right side of the canopy, the litter, still supported by *gaṇas* and attended by the flying horsemen, descends to earth, two *gaṇas* on tigers accompanying it, amidst a crowd of enthusiastic men, and applauding and laughing dwarfs. They have evidently surmounted the tree and canopy. In front are two empty high-backed chairs, and a piece of unsculptured stone, left probably to represent the top of a hill or rocky ground.

On the panel to the left, that is behind the castle gates from which the litter described above issues, part of another group is seen. A male figure leaning on a staff seems as if in the act of rising into the air. Three persons, standing, worship him. Others are below. In the foreground is a fainting female figure with women in attendance.

On the extreme right of the slab is another group. In the centre is Prince Siddhârtha, with a glory round his head, seated, surrounded by courtiers, with ladies seated on the ground below him. On the left, a man rushes off the scene in spite of forcible efforts to detain him made by some people who grasp his legs for the purpose.

All along the rounded coping above these sculptures is an inscription.

Mr. Fergusson assigns a Bactrian origin to the roll-ornament, and says, "Something at least very like it occurs among the sculptures at Jamâlgiri, near Peshawer, and "there so mixed with classical details as to make it appear much more ancient (p. 187)."[1] Possibly it had its origin in remote antiquity. In many places amongst the Egyptian hieroglyphs will be found representations of immensely long serpents. In one, depicted on p. 771 of the "*Monuments de l'Égypte et de la Nubie,*" of Champollion Le Jeune, the serpent is being supported by along row of priests, and is twisted into three folds between each. On the alabaster sarcophagus of Oimenepthah I., King of Egypt, is a representation of a long serpent spitting fire, doubled into folds just like the roll of the Buddhist frieze, and having a god standing on each fold, in the places occupied by the sacred emblems of the Buddhist faith in the friezes at Amarâvati. These designs are of course quite distinct, but they show us two principal ideas—an unnaturally long serpent carried by priests, and an unnaturally long serpent with objects of worship supported in

---

[1] In the "Graphic" newspaper of March 20th, 1880, appears an engraving representing Buddhist Antiquities found at Adah, four miles south of Jellalabad, in Afghanistan, by the Rev. C. Swinnerton, chaplain to the Khyber Force. Amongst these is conspicuous the roll-ornament supported by naked figures, having seated figures (Buddhas ?) in the folds, and for entablatures groups of five lotus-buds joined at their stalks. Adah is called "*Hi-lo*" by Fah-Hian and Hiouen-Thsang. (*See* Beal's "*Travels of Buddhist Pilgrims,*" p. 40; Julien's "*Vie de Hiouen-Thsang,*" p. 87; "*Memoires,*" i. 102, 135; ii. 188. And the same, ii. 304, for M. V. de St. Martin's remarks on the place, which he calls *Hiḍḍa*).

its vertical folds. These two ideas seem to be very often repeated in the Egyptian sculptures. If to the latter we add the former (viz., the priests supporting the weight of the folds) we should have exactly the roll-ornament. This may be considered too fanciful. But I would humbly submit that the Buddhist roll, which Mr. Fergusson says is to be seen in Burmah carried along in funeral processions to this day, and which probably is represented in these Amarávati friezes, may have had its origin in Western Asian or Egyptian ideas, where we find such designs as those I have described above on sepulchral monuments. The long roll may be intended to represent a serpent. As to the groups of emblems and worshippers, it is impossible not to be struck with the very close resemblance between the group of two worshippers adoring the *dharma chakra* on a pillar as we have it in these sculptures, and the oft repeated design found on Assyrian and Babylonian cylinders and seals, of priests or cherubim adoring an emblem which is sometimes taken to mean the sacred tree or grove, sometimes a wheel or sun-symbol on a pillar (George Smith's "*Chaldœan Account of Genesis*," pp. 89, 106. Bonomi, "*Nineveh and its Palaces*," p. 292).

Another point of interest here is the throne on the entablature of the roll. Nothing is so common on these sculptures as the representation of people adoring the throne or something on the throne. Constantly the object on the throne is something so indefinitely carved that it looks like a cushion, another such cushion being seen above. In the well preserved disc given in F., LXII. 1, the throne contains a sort of round tray with a small dagoba thereon, evidently a relic casket. Anything bearing on these points is of interest, and I therefore make no apology for reproducing here a passage from Fah Hian, describing what he saw at *Hi-lo* (Hiḍḍa or Aḍah, five miles south of Jellalabad in the Khyber):—

"Going westwards 16 yôjánas we arrive at the borders of the country of Na kie " (Nagrâk). In the city of Hi-lo is the Vihâra, containing the relic of the skull bone of " Buddha. This Vihâra is entirely covered with plates of gold, and decorated with the " seven precious substances. The king of the country reverences in a high degree this " sacred relic. For fear lest any man should carry off the true bone and substitute " another in its place, therefore he appoints eight persons belonging to the principal " families of the country to seal up (every night) the door of the shrine, each one with " his own seal, so as to guard and protect it. At early dawn these eight men all go to " the Temple, and each one observes if his seal is as he left it. They then open the door, " and having washed their hands with perfumed water, they take out the bone of Buddha " and place it upon a lofty throne which is erected outside the shrine. On this throne is " a circular table composed of the seven precious substances, with a crystal bell-shaped " cupola on the top. Both the table and the cover are highly decorated and enriched " with gems." Each day after the relic is so placed "certain men appointed for the " purpose ascend a lofty belfry and beat a great drum, blow the conch, and clash the " cymbals. When the king hears it he immediately repairs to the Vihâra and offers " flowers and incense; having done this, he repeatedly bends his head to the ground in " adoration and departs."

All this is completely rendered in the sculpture alluded to (F., LXII.), where the Dagoba on the throne is faithfully given.

The constant repetition of this design of the throne with something on it would give rise to the natural inference that it was customary, at those sacred places which boasted of a revered relic, for the priests to deal with it as Fah-Hian describes, and every day bring it forth and place it on a throne for adoration; and the sculptures at Amarávati may perhaps represent that daily exhibition of the object of worship (F., 197, 199, 200).

If so, it is not improbable that portions of this marble throne at Amarávati may hereafter be found.

The above twenty marbles are all that were lying wholly or in part exposed. They were all out of position, and are valuable only for the sculptures they bear.

I had set some workmen to excavate near the south point of the circle, thinking that as there was a cluster of stones there I might possibly hit on some others below ground, and I was not altogether disappointed, as four more were discovered. Their places (21 to 24 inclusive) will be seen noted on Plate II.

No. 21 was found lying 15 feet north-west of No. 4, and nearly on the same level. It was lying flat. (2 ft. 10 in. by 2 ft. 7 in.) It is a piece very similar to F., XCV., 1, 3, 4, but in far better preservation. Three figures remain, a Rajah and two women, but their heads are gone. The women have the immense twisted ankle ornaments that are seen disfiguring the lower limbs of the women in most of the Amarávati sculptures. It is hardly possible to imagine anything more barbarous and ungraceful. Underneath is the same diaper-pattern or rail-ornament band that appears on the other slabs similar to this. The back of the slab is plain and flat. (*It was photographed.*)

This slab belonging to the class included in Mr. Fergusson's elevation in Plate XCIII., I am again led to the question as to whether the central structure was a dagoba, 30 or 35 feet in diameter, or a domed tope of earth of the Sánchi type, and I would request attention to the native name for the place, *dipál-dinne*, or "*mound of lights.*"—Turning to General Cunningham's description of the *stupa* at Bharhut I find this passage (pp. 4, 5) relative to the central mound, a portion of the lower rim of which was discovered by him. "The lower half was quite plain, but the upper half was ornamented "with a succession of triangular shaped recesses, narrow at bottom and broad at top, "formed by setting back a few of the facing bricks. I conclude that these recesses "were intended for lamps[1] . . . . Each row would therefore have held 600 lamps "for an illumination. But as each row of these recesses would have given three lines of "lights, and as there were several rows of recesses the illumination would have taken "the form of a diamond-shaped network of lights covering the whole of the lower "part of the stûpa up to the spring of the Dome." Here there is a veritable "mound of lights" at Bharhut. And might not this term be used at Amarávati because there was something similar there? I cannot think that the term "*dinne*" could be applied to a marble dagoba (*see ante, note*, p. 23).

Before leaving the general question of the marbles of the central structure I must call to notice that in Mr. Fergusson's Plate XCV. (repeated of course on his Plate XCIII.) appear two stones, No. 1 and the lower half of No. 3. These are given as separate marbles, but in reality the photographs are of the two sides of the same marble. As in the case of one or two others, the sculptures have been executed on both sides. The side represented as No. 3 is infinitely better and more artistic than No. 1. Is the latter of an older date altogether? Or is it perhaps that a badly-executed sculpture was discarded, the slab reversed, and a better design carved on it by more skilled artists?

No. 22. (2 ft. 4 in. by 10 ft. 6 in.), (*photographed*).—A small fragment of the Outer-Rail coping-stone roll-ornament, similar in general design to that depicted in F., LVI., but smaller. It is more the size of F., XCII., 5, but differs from that in having no supporter. This stone, in fact, is a new variety of the rail coping. In the upper fold is a half-disc. In the lower, where the supporter usually is, are two lotus buds with intertwining stems. The whole is so much weatherworn that it is difficult to say whether the roll was ornamented with scroll-work and patterns as it usually is. It would seem not. Again, the square entablature, usually bearing some elaborate design, is here quite plain. Another peculiarity is that though the stone is evidently from its shape perfect, yet the reverse was never sculptured at all, but left blank. The curvature of the top is complete, proving that the back has not been broken off. At present it is impossible to say to what this slab belonged.

Exactly at the top was a square hole containing the remains of an iron pin, showing that the coping at that place was probably surmounted by some iron ornament (*see* F., p. 224).

The lotus-buds in the place of supporters are seen in a similar position on the roll frieze at Nassick.

---

[1] This style of wall facing, especially intended for illuminations, is seen at this day in India in numberless buildings. Mosques are hardly ever seen without them. And most of the private houses—at least those in villages on the Krishṇā—have them, especially for use at the "*Dîpâvali*," or Lamp-festival, in the autumn.

PLATE III.

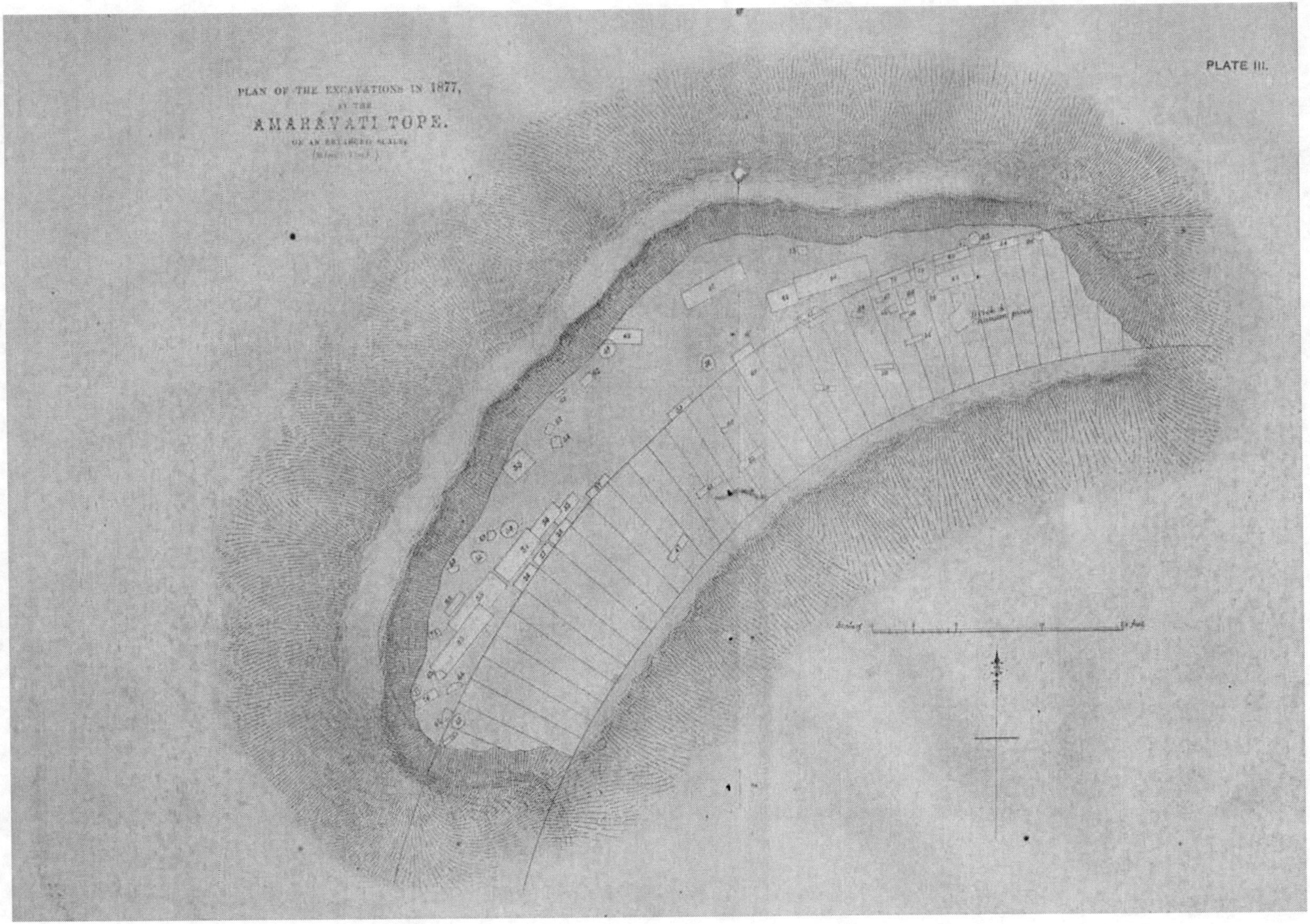
PLAN OF THE EXCAVATIONS IN 1877,
AT THE
AMARÁVATI TOPE.
ON AN ENLARGED SCALE

Nos. 23 and 24 are both fragments of the same portion of the building as my No. 21 and F., XCV. 1, 3, 4, XCVI. 1. Both were found close to the south point of the circle, but both quite out of position. These represent, apparently, each a sovereign with his queen. There are now seven of these in our possession. It is impossible, of course, to say where those figured by Mr. Fergusson were discovered, but the only three marbles bearing this subject unearthed by me were found lying just where the south gateway would have stood. In No. 23 (length 2 ft. 7 in., height 1 ft. 9 in.) only the feet and ankles of four figures remain, one man, and three women with heavy metal anklets. The back of the slab is blank, as are all of them. On a band below the figures is an inscription, and below this again the simple rail-ornament or diaper-pattern found on six out of the seven already discovered. In the case of No. 24 (3 ft. 7 in. by 2 ft.) the diaper band underneath the figures remains, but only the toes of three figures are visible above.

It was on the third day of our work that, on my return to the Tope from the Śiva Temple in the town where I had been taking notes of some sculptured slabs, the good news greeted me that the workmen had at last hit on the real platform between the rails. Hurrying to the spot I presently stood on the edge of the mound near its north-west point, and looked down on a yard or two of a dark stone flooring, quite different from the marble of which the sculptures are composed. This, undoubtedly, was the real platform, and, better still, it was at a point where in Colonel Mackenzie's time it had not been exposed, so that we might reasonably hope to find there a good crop of sculptures in fair preservation, and possibly part of the rail itself *in situ*. The results amply justified this hope, for in the next four days we discovered, examined, and catalogued 59 marbles, most of which were in infinitely better preservation than any of those exhibited in England.

My first care, having thus got a distinct base to work from, was to measure across the circle to ascertain where the platform on the other side might be expected to be found. The rails had an inner diameter of 165 feet, and a measurement of that length right across proved conclusively that on the opposite side of the circle the platform had been completely destroyed. Where it appears clearly marked at the south-east of Colonel Mackenzie's plan, there is now nothing. The four squared marbles that lay at E in my plan are not part of the platform. They are on a lower level altogether, and are 172 ft. 8 in. from the inner edge of the newly discovered platform. The real platform stones, too, are not marble.

The first slab that came to light on removing the earth from the platform was No. 25.

No. 25. A long slab having the roll ornament, but not, apparently, part of the Outer Rail (9 ft. 10 in. by 2 ft. 1 in.). It corresponds to F., XCII. 5. It has dwarfs for supporters, and half-discs in the folds of the roll; but the back is unsculptured. It has not been broken off, for the curvature of the top of the stone is seen to be complete, but it was left smooth and unsculptured.

I must mention that, when first discovered, No. 25 was lying flat on its face, the unsculptured side being uppermost, and that I left it exactly as it was till the removal of the earth about that part was complete and many other stones had been uncovered and noted. It was lying partly on the top of No. 35, and partly on earth. It was 3 feet above platform level.

Close to the north end of No. 25, the removal of the earth disclosed the tops of first one, then another, then a third stone, in such a position that it seemed probable that they were the lower portions of Outer Rail marbles still in position. This idea proved to be correct. 26 and 28 are the bases of pillars of the Outer Rail. 27 is the lowest of the three intermediate discs and is held in position by its flanges, which fit the mortices in the two pillars. I had these photographed *in situ*, and did not disturb them.

No. 26. Base of pillar of Outer Rail in position. The stone is 2 ft. 8 in. high by 2 ft. 3 in. broad. The base is let into the ground below the platform and outside it. For six inches above the platform the inner face of this slab is plain and smooth. Above this is a three-inch band of a sort of diaper pattern (*see* F., LIII. 2).

Then the half-disc, with its lotus-buds filling the corners. Above this the shaft is divided into three unornamented panels. It is important to notice that the back of this slab was never carved at all; it was smoothed, but unsculptured.

No. 27. Lotus-disc rail-bar of Outer Rail in position, its flanges fitting into the mortices in Nos 26 and 28 (2 ft. 9 in. broad by 2 ft. 4 in. high). It corresponds with the centre disc in F., LV. The back of this disc is plain and smoothed, but curved from top to bottom, as with the rail-bars at Sánchi. At Bharhut they are uncurved. Here and at Sánchi the curve follows the line of the lentil-shaped mortice. (Compare my No. 12, and No. 13 B.)

No. 28. (2 ft. 7 in. high by 2 ft. 2 in. broad.) Pair to No. 26, being the base of a second pillar of the Outer Rail, holding the flange of disc No. 27. It has a 3-inch flower-band across the base, 6 inches above platform level. Then the half-disc and buds. The pillar is divided into three unsculptured panels. The back is plain but smoothed, having no ornament whatever.

Right across the inside and sculptured face of these three erect marbles runs a line of brick and plaster work. What this was it is impossible to say, but it is clear that it was done at a time when the sculptures were held in very slight veneration.

There are several things to be noticed about these few marbles, the only ones beyond all question *in situ* discovered during my excavations. First of all I must mention that I did not disturb the earth outside the platform below the platform level; and it is necessary that this should be done, for Mr. Fergusson assigns to the outside base of the Outer Rail pillars, below the platform level, a zoöphorus or frieze of animals. Certainly fragments of such a frieze have been discovered, and if the rail at the Kenheri cave (woodcut 11, F., p. 92) is to be taken as our guide we should expect to find that frieze in position on the outside of these Amarávati Rails below the platform level. Besides this it is to be remembered that if Mr. Fergusson is correct, the existence of this lowest frieze about 2 feet high proves the ground level outside to have been originally 2 feet below the platform level; so that if the earth were excavated to that depth we might expect to find not only more marbles fallen out of position on to the then ground level, but, what would be of great interest and value, relics and perhaps coins dropped there in old times when the rails were first erected and before the ground outside them had begun to rise with the inevitable accumulations of years. It is precisely at that lowest level, and probably more thickly about the gateways, that treasures of great value to archæologists may be expected to be found. In the crush and bustle of festival days many coins might be expected to be dropped, bead necklaces unstrung, and ornaments broken, which would be trodden underfoot and lost in the dust and dirt in the crowds at the entrances. And I would therefore strongly urge the careful excavation and sifting of the earth down to that level; for a single coin found at the lowest level in good preservation may help to decide some chronological question at present doubtful.

Another point of interest connected with these three erect marbles is that the lowest point of the disc forming the rail bar is seen to be considerably below the position assigned to the lowest bars by Mr. Fergusson in his restoration, Plates XLVIII., XLIX. It rests almost on the platform level.

It will be noticed that the outsides of these marbles are quite plain and unsculptured, differing from many others which are sculptured on both sides; also that whereas, according to Mr. Fergusson's deductions from the pillars now at the India Museum, their inside faces between the lotus discs were richly ornamented, the outer having the shaft plain and simple, here the inner faces have the plain and simple shaft, the outer being unsculptured in any way. This affords additional proof, if any were needed, of how varied in design the different portions of the Rail were.

Throughout this paper I apply the term "half-disc" to the lotus ornaments not perfect circles, but it is deserving of remark that these are really *more* than half-discs in most instances, whereby the grace and elegance of the design is vastly increased. The inward sweep of the series of concentric rings below the true base of the semicircle increases beyond all expression the beauty of the curves.

About 4 feet above the level of these stones in the bank behind them was found the next fragment.

No. 29. (1 ft. 7 in. high by 1 ft. broad.) One of the *trisul* emblems from a cornice of similar ornaments (F., XCIII., XCVII.). It closely corresponds in style, size, and pattern of the band at its base with those seen in the lower right hand fragment of F., XCVII. It has been split off just above the animal frieze. (Photographed with Nos. 65 and 53.)

No. 30 was found close by the side of this in the bank.

No. 30. (3 ft. 3 in. by 1 ft. 6 in.) (Photographed with No. 9.) This is part of one of the flower-vases assigned by Mr. Fergusson to the base of the sculpture adorning the wall of the central building. (F., XCVI. 4.) Compare Nos. 9, 38, 58, 74.

Near these, but below them, and only three feet above the level of the platform were found the next three stones.

No. 31. One of the discs of the Outer Rail. In size, shape, and general design an exact pair to No. 27. The back is similarly curved in a smooth sweep from top to bottom.

As this was found so close to No. 27, which is the lowest of the three discs of the rail, it is not at all improbable that this marble was the upper or middle one between the same two uprights.

No. 32. (2 ft. 3 in. high by 7 in. broad.) A fragment I am unable to assign any position to. It is perfectly plain for most part of its surface, as also is the back; but near the top is a small figure of Buddha in a standing posture, 9 inches high, adored by worshippers. It bears an inscription.

No. 33. This is a marble interesting from its being one of a new class. There is none like it amongst the slabs at the British Museum. It measures 3 ft. 9 in. long by 3 ft. 3 in. high, and is a flat piece sculptured with the roll-ornament, but of little thickness. The whole height of 3 ft. 3 in. is taken up with the roll-frieze and the two flower-bands above and below, there being no symptom of the stone ever having had the rounded top which distinguishes the rail coping stones. And it will be observed that the entire frieze is several inches broader than any of the rail friezes. The back is plain, and the slab has all the appearance of having formed part of a flat sculptured wall. It was found lying flat on mud, 3 feet above platform level, the sculptured face uppermost.

The frieze has the roll-ornament, only one fold of which is seen. The emblem upheld by the fold is the empty throne, feet impressions, and *Dharma-chakra* with worshippers. The supporter is the usual draped figure. The square entablature on the roll has a wreathed dagoba.

On clearing away the earth from the back of the rail marbles in position (Nos. 26, 27, 28), three large slabs were found lying flat, their upper surfaces forming a sort of level flooring, their ends touching, apparently placed there deliberately. These were numbered 34, 35, 36. The flooring they form is a little higher than the level of the main platform. They were numbered, as were all the marbles, in order of their excavation, a process in some ways inconvenient but which is useful inasmuch as it shows the progress of the work.

No. 34 is a large slab, 6 ft. long by 2 ft. 8 in. broad. It evidently lay for long in its present position above ground and uncared for, as the flat unsculptured part of its upper surface was worked into holes for rice-pounding by the inhabitants of the neighbourhood. The same has been done with most of the flooring of the Uṇḍavilli rock-cut temple, 16 miles distant, and, it is reasonable to suppose, marks a period when the stone flooring remained perfectly uncovered and exposed but all veneration for the monument had ceased. It is one of the broader pillars of the Outer Rail, probably fallen or conveyed from a portion of the rail differing in size from that close to which it is found, where the pillars are only 2 ft. 3 in. broad. I left these large slabs as they lay without moving them, as I was anxious to get on with the uncovering of others during this period of work, and hoped to be able to return to finish the explorations on a future occasion. This slab is evidently the base of the pillar; 3 ft. 6 in. of its length is unsculptured. The remaining 2 ft. 6 in. is occupied by the flower-band, the lower half-disc, and a fragment of the sculptured three-panelled shaft. The centre division of this shaft bears a dagoba, and those on each side draperied worshippers, such as those seen in F., LVIII. 2.

No. 35 is a large slab lying underneath the heavy piece of rail coping No. 25. I did not remove No. 25, and was therefore unable to examine No. 35. The upper surface of the latter is quite smooth and plain; what the under surface bears remains to be seen.

No. 36. (3 ft. 3 in. long by 1 ft. 11 in. high.) This is a thin slab lying flat, its surface forming a flooring level with the surface of Nos. 34 and 35. Upper surface plain and unornamented. I did not have this raised till some other stones had been excavated, examined, and numbered. When it was raised it was found that another stone of smaller size had been placed underneath it, the two together being about the thickness of No. 34. I look upon this as almost conclusive that these stones were carefully *placed* in their present position for some purpose, smooth surfaces uppermost, and that they are not found as they fell from their true position on the structure. This No. 36, whose sculptured side was underneath as it lay, is one of the series forming an animal frieze which Mr. Fergusson assigns to the foot of the external face of the Outer Rail, F., XVII. This may be a correct conjecture, but my marble No. 45 should be examined in connexion with these, as the slab, though bearing a similar design, is rounded at the top like all the coping stones of the rail. No. 46 has a winged lion apparently ambling along. (In the specimens in the British Museum he is gallopping or trotting.) An attendant, dressed just like a "horsekeeper" of the present day, in short drawers and cloth with the ends flying out behind, holds him by the ear. He has a curved weapon in his left hand. Above this is a broad conventional flower-band with a *gaṇa*. Below is a stiff band of rather ugly diamond-shaped ornaments. I have a photograph of it for reference.

Continuing the clearing towards the north and round the outer edge of the platform, the workmen came to another portion of the base of an Outer Rail pillar in position, forming, with Nos. 26 and 28, three consecutive uprights. The disc between No. 28 and this has disappeared.

No. 37. Base of pillar of Outer Rail in position, forming, with Nos. 26 and 28, three consecutive supports of the rail.

The workmen, still clearing the earth in the same direction, took a line rather outside the curve of the platform, and next hit upon No. 38 which was lying on a mass of earth 2 feet above the level of the platform, proving how the mud had accumulated here before the slab fell, or was placed, where it was found.

No. 38. (2 ft. by 1 ft. 11 in.) Portion of one of the flower vases (*see* Nos. 9, 30, 58, 74) forming, according to Mr. Fergusson, the base of the sculptures which decorated the surface of the central dagoba. It is in all respects similar to the others, and needs no separate notice.

Very shortly after hitting on No. 38 the coolies found No. 39, which is another fragment in position, or to all appearance so, on the outer edge of the platform—part, in short, of the Outer Rail.

No. 39. (2 ft. 6 in. high by 2 ft. 7 in. broad.) I regret that I am unable to give as accurate a description of this slab as I should wish. The stone is an interesting one, and should be more carefully examined. I can only quote verbatim the note I made of it on the spot:—"Pillar *in situ*. Inside is the same as 26, 28, but the "back is carved with half-disc and flower-band with dolphins' heads at the ends. "The back is slightly curved. Behind this is a broken stone imbedded in the "ground close up against it."

A reference to the plan, and observation of the positions of stones 40 to 46 inclusive, will show how our excavations proceeded, working back into the high mound in rear of the platform. As each stone appeared I marked it, postponing its thorough examination till the earth was cleared away. No. 40 was lying flat on a mass of earth 2 ft. 8 in. above platform level. I did not move it from position because it is useful to show that the structure was not all demolished at one time.

No. 40. (6 ft. 1 in. long by 2 ft. 6 in. broad.) Apparently the base of a pillar of the Outer Rail, external face uppermost. It has the lower half-disc on a plain diaper-pattern band. Above this, the shaft, though divided into three panels, is not further ornamented. The lower portion of the central disc remains, the rest having been broken away.

This stone requires more careful examination, and it is especially necessary to see from its position whether it is really a pillar of the Outer Rail fallen inwards, or whether it formed part of any other portion of the Tope.

Close in rear of this was lying, in a slanting position but with its base still imbedded apparently as it stood, No. 41, the lower part of a pillar of the outer rail.

No. 41. Above a few inches of plain unsculptured base is a flower-band, above which is the usual half-disc and lotus buds. From the base of the flower-band 5 feet of sculpture remains. This stone is interesting because, though the middle disc has the lotus pattern, like the external face of these pillars (F., L., LI., LII., LIII.), the three compartments between it and the lower half-disc are sculptured with groups of figures, as on the internal face of the pillars seen in F., LVIII., LIX., LX., LXI. This stone is therefore a variety. From its position it would seem that the face bearing the sculptures now under notice was *outside.* What was inside will probably never be known, as the slab has been split down its entire breadth, and the inner face broken off. The centre panel of the shaft above the lower half-disc has a group of five men and a child collected round a white-ants' nest,[1] feeding the cobra it contains with milk (?) from a dish. Above them is a bo-tree. All concerned seem smiling and pleased. The left panel is much broken away, but a prince on a throne with attendants is seen. He does not appear to be Siddhârtha, for he has no nimbus round his head. In the left compartment is a man dancing in an excited attitude, and holding up his waist-cloth.

Close in rear of this was the upper portion of a rail pillar, No. 42. A very heavy slab, No. 46, which will presently be described, was on top of its lower end, though about a foot higher in the ground, and as I did not remove this from its position (except to raise it for photographic purposes), the complete examination of No. 42 was postponed. The upper portion, however, which is visible, proves it to be the top of one of the pillars, and of an interesting variety, as the uppermost half-disc, instead of being simply carved in the lotus design, has a group of figures in the centre.

No. 42. Upper portion of a pillar of the Outer Rail, with apparently the inside face uppermost (breadth 2 ft. 7 in., length not known as part was left imbedded). At the top is a frieze of animals, tigers, wolves, lions, and bears, with a *gaṇa* at each end. The upper half-disc has a group of worshippers, prostrate and adoring, below a bo-tree with Buddha's feet impressions underneath; the whole surrounded by a double band, the inner having the lotus leaf design, the outer a wreath of flowers. The shaft underneath is divided as usual into three panels, of which the right only can as yet be seen. It has a man with a snake twisted round his arm, and a woman with a *chaori*.

Behind these slabs, 7 or 8 feet from the platform, and 1 foot above platform level, lay No 43, a slab belonging to the Outer Rail coping. It is unsculptured on its upper surface. When raised it split into several pieces, a misfortune possibly due to its great age, as it certainly seems to belong to one of the older parts of the rail. The curvature of the top is complete, proving that the back was purposely left smooth and unsculptured.

No. 43. (9 ft. 4 in. by 2 ft.) One of the old rail coping stones, bearing the roll ornament, which in its folds supports half lotus-discs. The slab is so weatherworn that it does not appear what the supporters of the roll were. It has a few letters of an inscription in a style certainly older than the characters on many other of the marbles. (Compare F., XCII. 5 and my No. 22.)

---

[1] This is, I think, similar in design to that in the right-hand panel of the shaft of the pillar given in F., LX. Mr. Fergusson thinks that the cobra is issuing from a "curiously constructed cell," p. 193, but it is more probably intended for a white-ant heap, a favourite haunt of snakes in India.

In the bank behind No. 43 were found, about 1 ft. 6 in. above platform level, the next two numbers, close together, No. 45 lying in a slanting position on top of No. 44 which was flat.

No. 44. Disc of the Outer Rail. In size and design it is exactly similar to Nos. 27, 31.

No. 45 is a very interesting stone. I have alluded to it when describing No. 36. This fragment has a man and a bull, and a man and a stag, exactly similar in style to the sculptures on No. 36, and on Mr. Fergusson's Plate LVII. But whereas those slabs appear to be, like No. 36, thin and flat, and are consequently assigned by him to a frieze below the external face of the Outer Rail, this No. 45 is a coping stone, curved at the top like the roll-ornament coping stones of the Outer Rail, to which it assimilates in everything but the sculpture on its face. No other such slab has been found, all the other coping-stones having the roll ornament. This one introduces an entirely new feature.

No. 46 is a very handsome slab in good preservation. As before mentioned, it was found lying with its end resting on No. 42, about a foot of earth intervening.

No. 46. (8 ft. 9 in. long by 2 ft. 8 in. high.) (Inner face photographed.) Coping-stone of the Outer Rail in excellent preservation.

On the outer face is the roll ornament, of which there are five folds seen. The supporters are those usually seen in that position, but here each one is assisted by a diminutive female. The place of honour in the central fold of the roll is held by a *garuḍa* holding a five-headed *nâga* in his beak, as in the right hand upper fragments in F., LVI. (*see his pp.* 187, 188). The outer folds have a bo-tree, and a dagoba shaded by a cloud of umbrellas and having for its principal figure a five-headed cobra. In the remaining folds are a tower with three dwarfs on its summit, and a group of three *gaṇas* holding a sort of dish from which rise three horses. The square entablatures on the roll are considerably weatherworn; two of them have arabesque ornaments; on others are figures, but they are barely distinguishable.

The principal object of worship in the central panel of the inner face of this stone is the empty throne and feet impressions of Buddha, overshadowed by the bo-tree and umbrellas. A dish of offerings lies in front of the throne, and a number of people are grouped around. On the left are seen two women, each with a female attendant. With the woman nearest the throne is a boy, the other holds a little girl. Below them a prostrate female adores the sacred symbols. On the right is a somewhat stout prince with an attendant, in front of whom are three seated figures in atitudes of respect. Above are a number of flying figures, male and female, and dwarfs.

On the right of the slab is a castle. In a room above is seen an empty throne with five persons seated round it. Below, a recumbent female on her couch with her child by her side, to whom two female attendants are paying great attention. A horseman rides out from the castle and is about to pass through a *toraṇ* gateway similar to those at Sánchi, but his progress is stopped by a figure who seizes the horse's bridle; two attendants being behind, and a *gaṇa* in the air above. (Or it may be that the rider has just mounted his horse, the figure holding the reins being the groom. This would seem most probable, judging from his costume of short drawers). On the roof of the castle is an inscription.

On the left is seen the garden of the palace with a queen seated, apparently pensive and sad. Many female attendants are near her, and musicians, and one brings her a dish of food (?), as if through a gateway. The attitude of the principal figure is one of dejection. In the balcony of the palace is another female.

Further to the left again, and not seen in the photograph on account of No. 41 coming in the way, is the inside of a palace showing five rooms. In one is a woman playing an instrument. In another a woman is seated in an attitude of thought with her head on her hand. In a third two women are seen gossipping. In the two lower compartments are men in conversation, and a prince seated and talking to five courtiers who are grouped around him. He does not seem to be Siddhârtha, as he has no *nimbus* round his head.

Below these sculptures is a band of lions and flowers.

The central panel probably represents a historical subject, though it may be difficult to identify it. The prince's stout figure, and the boy and girl worshippers, renders this probable. As to the group on the right, at first sight I took it to be the departure of Prince Siddhârtha from his palace, with his groom *Chandaka*, and his horse *Kantaka*, the empty throne in the palace above typifying that it was the prince himself who was riding forth. But the surrounding figures render this impossible, for they are all awake and occupied, whereas the legend declares that at the time of Siddhârtha's departure the Devas had plunged all the inhabitants of the castle into a mysterious and profound sleep. Moreover the recumbent princess has a child by her side, whereas Yasodhara's child, Rahula, was not born for six years after the prince's flight. It is possible that the three subjects represent separate events; (1) the young Siddhârtha, reverenced by the women, lying by his mother, Máyá's, side, during one of the seven days preceding her death; (2) Siddhârtha grown up and quitting the palace to become the Buddha; the scene (3) above typifying the emptiness of the palace after his departure. The group in the garden on the left may well represent Yasodharâ deserted, lonely, and sad, after her husband's departure, attended by women who in vain try to raise her spirits. The other subjects I am at present unable satisfactorily to identify. In the palace scene on the extreme left the prince does not seem to be Siddhârtha, for he is not represented with a glory round his head, and he is too old for the boy Rahula.

Mr. Fergusson comments (pp. 187, 188) on the curious fact of the *Nâga,* who is an object of worship or at least superstitious reverence in these sculptures, being here represented as in the grasp of a conquering *Garuḍa.* He considers it probable that the symbol relates in some way to the antagonism of Vaishnavism and Buddhism. It is worth while observing that amongst the Buddhist legends given by Spence Hardy in his "Manual of Buddhism," pp. 302–3, is the following story of the *Nága Nandópananda* being overcome by *Mugalán* in the form of a *garuḍa*:—

"At the time that Budha visited the déwa-lóka Tawutisá, the nága king, Nandópananda, said to his subjects, 'The sage, Gótama Budha, has passed over the world on his way to 'Tawutisá; he will have to return by the same way again, but I must try to prevent his 'journey.' For this purpose he took his station upon Maha Méru. When one of the priests who accompanied Buddha, Rathapála, said that he had often passed in that direction before, and had always seen Maha Méru, but now it was invisible, Budha informed him that it was the Nága Nandópananda who had concealed the mountain. Upon hearing this, Rathapála said that he would go and drive him away; but the sage did not give him permission. Then Mugalan offered to go and subdue the nága, and having obtained leave, he took the form of a snake, and approached Nandópananda. The nága endeavoured to drive him to a distance by a poisonous blast, but Mugalan sent forth a counterblast, and there was a battle of blasts, but the blast of the priest was more powerful than that of the nága. Then the nága sent forth a stream of fire, and Mugalan did the same, by which he greatly hurt the nága, whilst the other stream did no injury whatever to himself. Nandópananda said in anger, 'Who art thou that attackest me with a force sufficient to 'cleave Maha Méru?' And he answered, 'I am Mugalan.' After this he went in at one ear of the nága, and out at the other; then in at one nostril, and out at the other; he also entered his mouth, and walked up and down in his inside, from his head to his tail, and from his tail to his head. The nága was still further enraged by this disturbance of his intestines, and resolved to squeeze him to death when he emerged from his mouth, but Mugalan escaped without his perceiving it. Another poisonous blast was sent forth, but it did not ruffle a single hair of the priest's body. After this Budha imparted to Mugalan the power to overcome the nága, and taking the form of a garunda, he began to pursue him; but Nandopananda offered him worship, and requested his protection."

While completing the examination of these sculptures my workmen were clearing the platform of earth, and we found several loose stones, 47 to 52 inclusive, lying on it.

No. 47. (3 ft. 4 in. long by 9 in. high.) Piece of a small cornice having alternate Buddhas (with nimbus) seated on lotus thrones, and dagobas wreathed with many umbrellas.

No. 48 is a fragment, similar, but of larger dimensions, the designs being separated into distinct panels by vertical lines (3 ft. 10 in. by 10 in. high). It is less elaborately sculptured. It has a small inscription in small letters apparently of a later date than those on many others.

These pieces of cornice seem new. The only specimen like them that I can find amongst the marbles now in England is to be seen in F., XCVI. 1, under the principal figure group. But even that is only similar in *style*. Both these new specimens have been photographed.

No. 49 (4 ft. long by 9 in. high) is apparently a portion of the same cornice as No. 47 in style and size. But, as if in proof that this cornice belonged to some later building, I find that this piece has been sculptured on the side of an older broken pillar, which had a half disc on it. This and the style of the letters of the inscription on No. 48 corroborate one another as to the later date of these stones.

No. 50 (1 ft. 8 in. by 9 in.) is another small piece of the same.

No. 51 (2 ft. 9 in. by 9 in.) is another. Underneath this fragment are remains of lentil-shaped mortices of small size for the the tenons of rail discs, as if this cornice had been sculptured on a broken fragment of a rail pillar. But this rail, if such is the case, and supposing it to be similar in design to the principal outer rail of the Tope, would be only 4½ ft. high, as the mortice is only 1 ft. long and four inches broad at the broadest. All along this stone is an inscription, of which I have a very poor impress.

No. 52 is a very fine stone in excellent preservation, one of the most beautiful yet found amongst these marbles. It is a portion of the elaborately sculptured frieze placed by Mr. Fergusson at the top of the Inner Rail (F., LXXV., LXXXII., LXXXIII.), and described by him on p. 223–5. I have a very poor and ill-focussed photograph of it which does not do it justice.

It measures 5 ft. 1 in., by 1 ft. 5 in. in height.

As in F., LXXXII. 1, the design consist of scenes divided by three elaborately sculptured bosses or lotuses placed one above the other, each scene being separated from the other by a pair of larger figures or a Buddha. In the left panel is a prince, apparently leaving some place in spite of the entreaties of a boy who pleads with him. A *gaṇa* shews the way, and behind the prince is a *toraṇ* gateway. In the background is a woman seemingly aged, and with a dejected expression. To the right of these a prince sits conversing, and surrounded by a number of females. In his hands he holds a string or cloth. Four of the women are seated on the low basket-work chairs so common in these sculptures, and on the ground below one of these is a little child. It is apparently this group which the prince on the left is leaving. The woman seated on the right has a sort of dish in her hands containing some object.

To the right of the three dividing discs are two standing figures, male and female, fully draped. The female seems to offer the male a cup. The male has a staff in his hands. This may represent Sujátá's milk-offering to Buddha on his leaving the forest before his contest with Mára; and this seems most probable from the fact of the female offering the male a cup-like vessel, while a vase is seen on the ground below.

The next panel to the right shews us another subject, apparently historical, but which I cannot identify. A prince, seated on a throne with his wife, and surrounded by females, is violently urged to action by a number of armed men with spears and swords. One soldier seems actually about to drag the prince off his throne by his waist-cloth. The object of attack is seemingly away to the left, in which direction some are moving and many looking. Behind is seen a *toraṇ* gateway. With the group below the throne is a little child.

To the right of this is Buddha enthroned and surrounded with the nimbus in the attitude of teaching. Two females are seen in attendance and two *gaṇas* in adoration.

Next to this are a number of men and women dancing excitedly in extravagant attitudes. What the object of their adoration is cannot be seen as the slab is here broken off, but the group seems similar to that in F., LXXIII. 2.

The bosses or discs are beautifully executed, the circular centre of several of them being sculptured with small figures only an inch high, but apparently carefully executed. These however are weatherworn.

Under the little braided band that runs along the bottom of this frieze is a cornice elaborately sculptured with a series of animals and men, so placed that they could be well seen from below; additional proof that Mr. Fergusson is correct in placing these slabs at a high level, they being almost invisible when the slab is viewed only at the height of the eye. The animals are a dolphin; a lion; a man running; a bull; a man seizing a galloping bull by the horn; another threatening a running stag; a third stopping a camel by frightening it; a man forcibly stopping a rhinoceros; a man striking a lion; another stopping some animal that has been broken off; two men stopping an elephant, one at its head, the other grasping its leg; a man stopping a lion which leaps on to him; a man running from a lion which pursues him; and a man forcibly arresting a bull while another lifts the animal's tail.

Each of these animals is about three inches long and an inch and a half high. They are cut in high relief, the whole forming not only a very elegant band, but testifying to the wonderful patience and skill of the workmen who executed the slab.

The supporters of the cornice are mythical figures with protruding breasts, and heads of lions, birds, and women.

Below this is an inscription, having letters apparently corresponding with those on F., LXXXIII. 1.

The legend of Sujátá alluded to in the above description is as follows. She was the daughter of Sénáni, a noble who resided near Uruwel, and just at the time when Siddhârtha was about to quit the forest she prepared some rice-milk with great skill, putting it into a golden vessel with a golden cover, and carried it to the prince. When she offered the food Siddhârtha found that his almsbowl had vanished. Sujátá thereupon "took off the cover of the vessel and presented it to him as an almsbowl." (Hardy's *Manual of Buddhism*, p. 168.) The story, as given in the *Abhinishkramana Sutra* (Beal's "*Romantic History of Buddha*," 193–94), varies in some degree, but is substantially the same.

While the clearance of the platform was still going on we discovered the stone lying under No. 36, which I have referred to when describing that one. This I numbered 53.

No. 53. (2 ft. 4 in. by 1 ft. 4 in.) This is a fragment of the base of a small pillar having the half-disc on two of its sides, and somewhat similar to F., XC. 6. But it has been used to form part of the face of a building, its side being carved. It has a double band with a rail-pattern ornament. In the space above are three knobs like large nail heads. There is no other stone yet found having any sculpture like this, and I cannot assign it to any position at the Tope.

Amongst the débris on the platform, and close to the large slabs 41 and 46, was found No. 54.

No. 54. (1 ft. 9 in. by 9 in.) A fragment of the same portion of the rail as Nos. 36, 45, and F., LVII. It has the conventional flower-band with two birds.

At this stage of the work my attention was directed to the east side of the circle, where, on turning the pillar (No. 17) which lay outside the east gate, a fragment (No. 55) was found underneath it.

No. 55. (1 ft. 11 in. by 9 in.) A very clear cut well preserved fragment of one of the lotus-discs of the rail. I had this photographed, but my artist does not do it justice.

Returning to the main clearings I found some more stones come to light. No. 56 was found amongst the débris close to No. 54.

No. 56. (1 ft. 4 in. by 5 in.) A small fragment of a pillar. It is apparently to be assigned to the Inner Rail, being like No. 72.

Some small stones were now turned out of the high mound in rear of the outer rail stones 26, 27, 28, 37 and these I numbered continuously. (No. 60 was lying on the platform near No. 40.)

No. 57. (1 ft. 4 in. by 4 in.) Portion of one of the *trisul* emblems, which formed the uppermost member of the main decoration of the Central Dagoba according to Mr. Fergusson's theory. (*See* F., XCIII. and my No. 29.)

No. 58 is a fragment of a piece similar to Nos. 9, 30, 38, 74.

No. 59. (1 ft. 3 in. by 8 in.) Fragment of one of the lotus-discs of the Outer Rail.

No. 60. (6 in. by 8 in.) A portion of sculpture, unassignable, having a Buddha.

No. 61. (10 in. by 4 in.) A small portion of the base of the elaborately sculptured cornice forming the coping of the Inner Enclosure (F., LXXXII., and my No. 52). This has a portion of the inscription which ran along under the sculpture, and of the small underlying cornice and supporters at the foot of the main cornice. The letters of the inscription are very small, not more than one-third of an inch high, and partake of the same character as those on No. 52.

No. 62. (1 ft. 10 in. by 7 in.) This is a fragment of the roll frieze of the Outer Rail and corresponds to No. 43 and F., XCII. 5. A *gaṇa* supports the roll.

On removing the earth from the southern portion of the mound at the back of and covering the platform, we exposed the whole surface of the long rail slab 25, and found a small stone (63) resting on its southern extremity.

No. 63. (1 ft. 5 in. by 5 in.) A fragment of sculpture so broken that it is impossible to determine to what it belonged. It is a well executed group, apparently one of the domestic palace scenes so common on these marbles. A portion of the enthroned prince is seen with a woman (princess?), in a somewhat loving manner encircling with her arm the lower part of the prince's couch. Below is a portion of an ornamental band of flowers.

Close to this last was found No. 64.

No. 64. (1 ft. 2 in. by 10 in.) A fragment of the lower portion of a pillar having parts of the flower-band and lower half-disc.

The workmen who were engaged in clearing the earth from the platform to the north of the newly excavated portion found three more marbles lying on the platform near its outer edge (Nos. 65, 66, 67).

No. 65. (1 ft. 10 in. by 1 ft. 4 in.) A fragment of sculpture having, on a flower band, a number of persons adoring an enthroned Buddha, only a small piece of whose figure is seen. This may belong to the internal face of the upper frieze of the outer rail, or it may be one of those fragments assigned by Mr. Fergusson to the central dagoba. (*Photographed.*)

No. 66. (2 ft. 7 in. by 1 ft. 10 in.) Half of a lotus-disc rail-bar, similar to the others.

No. 67. (1 ft. by 1 ft.) This is a small fragment, apparently part of the plinth of some portion of the building, but it is much weatherworn and cannot at present be accurately assigned to any part of the Tope. It has the remains of an inscription in large letters, but of a type certainly not the oldest amongst those found on these marbles.

Two more stones (68, 69) were next found, amongst the earth at the southern clearance.

No. 68. (2 ft. 8 in. by 1 ft. 6 in.) This is a fragment which I think must have formed part of the sculptures of the western gate. It is a slab having a graceful female figure with hand on hip leaning against a tree, in attitude somewhat similar to that of the dancers or tree-devas, under the beams of the *toraṇ* gateways at Sánchi. There is none like it amongst the marbles yet found at Amarávati.

No. 69. (Diameter 2 ft. 9 in.) A disc of the Outer Rail. In this instance the disc is sculptured with a figure group. It therefore would be placed by Mr. Fergusson as the central disc of the three between the pillars. The back has been split off. It was probably carved with the usual lotus ornament. The sculptured design is one which I cannot identify. It represents a forest or side of a rocky hill, filled with wild animals. There is a pond in the foreground at the base of the design, represented, as usual, by flowers growing in it. Round this are several elephants, one of whom is drinking. He has filled his trunk with water, and is discharging the contents into his mouth. Other elephants, old and young, are shewn amongst the rocks, with a deer, a wild boar, some birds, and two tigers. At the back, *i.e.*, quite at the top of the sculpture, is a man carrying two loads by a stick slung over his shoulder. I have had this photographed.

About 200 yards from the Tope, between it and the old fort of Dharaṇikóṭa, in a clump of trees, is a stone revetted well with steps down to the waterside, and it was pointed out to me that many fragments of marbles from the Tope were to be seen there. I accordingly made a careful examination of the place, and found a considerable number of remains from the stûpa utilised for steps and revetment. It would be difficult to reclaim all these, because it would entail considerable expense in replacing them with other stones. I saw a beautifully smooth and polished flat slab with a circular front, which looked as if it had been carved for the resting-place of a statue, or the steps of a throne. This forms one of the steps down to the water. Close to this is a piece with a clear cut Páli inscription under an ornamental band, having letters of lesser antiquity than some at the stûpa.

Three marbles easy to remove I carried away and placed amongst those at the mound, afterwards conveying them to the Bezwada Museum where they now lie. These I numbered 70, 71, 72, and had them photographed.

No. 70. (2 ft. 2 in. by 1 ft. 1 in.) This is a beautiful and well-preserved fragment from one of the dagobas of the Inner Enclosure. The figures, standing out with all the clear relief of ivory carvings, are only about 3 inches high. In the upper portion is an enthroned Buddha, with disciples.

No. 71 is one of the Inner Enclosure pillars, 5 ft. high by 1 ft. 1 in. broad. It represents the *chakra* ("*Dharma-chakra*," or "wheel of the Law;" *query*, sun-emblem ?) supported on a pillar, with figures and horses in excited attitudes rising from it on either side. (F., LXXV.)

No 72 (1 ft. 10 in. by 7 in.) is another similar fragment, but smaller. It is the top of a small pillar of the same design.

From the high mound at the back of the platform at the stûpa, close to No. 46, the large flat slab already described, we found part of a head of Buddha sculptured in bas-relief. This I numbered 73.

No. 73. The upper portion of a head of Buddha, larger than life, showing the short hair curling to the right. It is sculptured in bas-relief on what probably was a flat marble slab.

This is one of those stones that cannot yet be assigned to any known portion of the stûpa, and it is useless to theorize till all the excavations are complete.

The next stone was found amongst the clearances at the north side of the platform itself.

No. 74. (1 ft. 8 in. by 1 ft.) A portion of one of the flower-vase wall ornaments, like Nos. 9, 30, 38, 58.

The next three were found in the bank at the southern end of the platform clearances.

No. 75. (1 ft. 6 in. by 1 ft. 1 in.) A fragment of sculpture, unassignable at present, representing Buddha holding a bo-tree. It is awkward and conventional, and by no means so artistic as the great bulk of these sculptures.

No. 76 (*a* and *b*). Two portions—*a* the lower, *b* the upper—of one of the older Outer Rail coping-stones. Like No. 25 and F., XCII. 5, this has the roll-ornament upheld by *gaṇas*. *A* is 3 ft. 9 in. long by 11 in. broad, and shows us only the diaper-pattern band running along under the base of the frieze. *B*, measuring 3 ft. 6 in. by 6 in. broad, is the upper portion of the same. The central part has not yet been found.

No. 77 is a disc of the Outer Rail having the lotus ornament, with a diameter of 2 ft. 7 in. The back is split off.

The workmen at the northern clearance now came upon a series of slabs lying along the outer edge of the platform at that part, which I was anxious to uncover, the earth there not being so deep as at the southern end, and our time for work running short. We therefore concentrated our energies on this point and succeeded in laying bare seven more marbles, 78 to 84 inclusive. Their positions will be seen in the plan.

No. 78. (3 ft. 6 in. by 2 ft. 7 in.) One of the ends of the roll-ornament on the Outer Rail coping. This is an interesting piece of sculpture of a distinctively humorous character. In other marbles, where the end of the roll is shown, we see it being swallowed by *makaras* or fish monsters as in my No. 1 and F., XCII. 4. But in this there is a quaint and original element introduced. The supporting figures are here seen with eager and excited gestures laughingly cramming the roll down the throat of an unfortunate *gaṇa*, who is almost too big for the frieze. He is sitting helpless, his great overgrown body swelled to excess by the masses of roll which he is evidently supposed to have swallowed already; his head jammed against the top of the frieze; an expression of ludicrous dismay and distress on his face; while he is held in position for the operation by a small female who grasps his ear. This is certainly the most comical bit I have seen amongst the sculptures yet excavated. There is something like it—the same idea —at Sánchi (*see* F., VIII.), on the central portion of the lower beam above the southern gateway; but there, as would appear from the drawing, the *gaṇas* at each end seem quite contented at what they are doing. Here the poor dwarf's helpless terror is admirably shown. Above the fold of the roll is a group of three elephants supporting a slab with a small flower-vase sculptured on it.

The reverse or internal face of the slab has a figure sculpture. In the centre is seen a castle wall with high gates. Outside the castle are five men with an elephant, and in attendance on them a *gaṇa*. Inside the castle is seen a prince seated with two women (his wives?), having other women in attendance fanning him.

The slab bears an inscription in very clear characters of a somewhat late date, the ends of the letters being much rounded. The vowel *ĭ* form is developed into a bold sweep upwards, with a reverse curve at the end.

I submitted this inscription to Dr. Burnell, as being one of the clearest of those found at the stûpa, and I quote *in extenso* his note on it:—

" *-kayas(s)a ku(?)ligāya-mahā-cetiye ut(t)arāyāke unisa-dāna(n).*

" of (by) . . . kaya, in the great Kuligāya caitya, in the northern ?, a gift of a crown.

" There are many difficulties here. *Kuligāya* may be a proper name. *Ut(t)arāyakam* is clearly a technical term, as is also *unisa*. This last may be for Sk.*ushṇīsha*, but the correct form would then be *uṇhisa*, or something like it. It may mean (if this derivation is accepted) a crown, stairs, or perhaps coping of a wall, &c."

The original must be more carefully examined. For the question suggests itself whether the word which in my impress reads doubtfully *kuligāya* may possibly be *kaliṅgāya*, "the great chaitya of Kalinga"? As to *utarāyāke*, *uttara-āya* in Sanskrit would be "the northern entrance." Can there be any such meaning here? The slab was found close to the spot where the northern gate would have stood, and is probably the end of the frieze of the rail at that point. *Uṇhīsam* in Páli means "a crest, diadem, crown; a turban; part of a staircase" (Childers). If it might mean *a coping stone*, that would exactly apply to this slab.

The whole would then be "gift of a coping stone at the northern entrance of the great chaitya of Kalinga by . . . kaya."

"No. 79 (3 ft. 6 in. by 1 ft. 8 in.) is a portion of an Outer Rail pillar, with the back broken off. The remaining sculpture is that of its inner face. On the band along the top is an animal frieze having pairs of lions and bulls. Below this is the upper half-disc, with a flower-band round it. Below this again is the usual three-panelled shaft, the central compartment of which has a figure group of a prince seated with his wife, and a woman in front apparently making a petition. The compartment to the right is broken. That on the left has a prince seated, with attendants.

No. 80 (4 ft. by 1 ft. 9 in.) is a much injured portion of the Outer Rail coping.

The outer face is so much broken that only a fragment of the roll-ornament is seen, and of the band below it with flowers and animals.

On the much weatherworn inner face can be seen a figure close to a pond with lotus flowers growing in it. To the right of this, in a garden with buildings scattered about, are three persons apparently worshipping another who is seated feeding a bird. I have no photograph of this, and I cannot say from memory whether or not it is likely to represent the legend of King Śivi, but I think not.

No. 81. (1 ft. 9 in. by 1 ft. 1 in.) I cannot recall this to my recollection. My note says, "Fragment. Boys playing with a bull who charges."

No. 82. (4 ft. by 2 ft. 10 in.) Another portion of the Outer Rail roll-ornament coping. The emblem in the fold of the roll is a dagoba with attendant worshippers. On the entablature on the roll itself is Buddha's throne and feet impressions, and the "wheel of the law" with worshippers.

The inner face has two scenes. That on the left has Buddha, shown by the nimbus round his head, seated under a tree and surrounded by five persons. Another tree is behind. The place is evidently a garden or forest. The compartment on the right has six persons worshipping some one. The stone is here broken. The object of their adoration is probably Buddha.

It seems natural to suppose that the representation of Buddha amongst trees with five companions is intended to portray him during his six years asceticism in the Uruwela Forest with the five Brahmans, Kondanya, Bhaddaji, Wappa, Mahánámá, and Assaji. (Hardy's "*Manual of Buddhism*," p. 165.) Possibly it may be the garden of the Jetavana Monastery.

No. 83. Lotus-disc of Outer Rail, having the lotus-ornament on both sides. One side shows a variety of this design, the disc being slightly concave instead of convex. (2 ft. 9 in. diam.)

No. 84 is the central portion of a pillar of the Outer Rail showing the outer and inner faces of the middle disc. The external face has the usual lotus ornament, but in this case rather heavy and awkward. On the internal face, within a circle of flowers, is the empty throne of Buddha and his feet impressions, behind which is a pillar richly ornamented supporting the *dharma-chakra*. On each side are 12 worshippers. The diameter of this disc is 2 ft. 9 in., corresponding in size to F. LVIII. 1.

Another small fragment was found at the south clearance just on the platform.

No. 85. Fragment of a pillar. Unimportant.

The last stone which I attempted to note, No. 86, was found just on the outer edge of the platform at the clearance to the north.

No. 86. (10 in. by 11 in.) A fragment probably broken off the base of the internal face of one of the Outer Rail coping slabs. It has two draped figures standing on a flower band, but only the legs of the figures appear.

By the time these marbles had been unearthed my time was expended, and my ordinary official work compelled me to leave Amarávati, and return to head-quarters. I was therefore reluctantly compelled to abandon the work of excavation at a time when it was especially interesting from the number of sculptured marbles that were constantly being found. It was on the morning of the 1st of May that the workmen hit on the platform, and by the evening of the 5th we had removed a mound, varying from 12 ft. to 2 ft. in depth, on a space having a greatest length of 94 ft. and a greatest breadth of 29½ ft. In this space were found and completely uncovered 59 marbles, some of large size and some in very beautiful preservation, far surpassing any of those now in England. But this was not all, for a number of other stones were discovered in the mound at the southern end of the clearance, and if more time had been at my disposal these also would have been completely excavated and reported on. As it was I saw no better course to adopt than to have them covered again with earth, shovelled down from the top of the mound so as to hide them. The locality being known they could always be found when wanted, and the sloping off of the mound would to a certain extent prevent those already discovered from being injured. This was accordingly done.

Besides these 86 marbles at the stûpa itself, a large number can be seen, as I have already mentioned, let into the walls and towers of the handsome temple dedicated to Śiva under the title of *Amaréśvara-swami*, on the river bank about a quarter of a mile north of the stûpa. These are I fear irrecoverable, as the masonry work is built on them. It must not be supposed that they were selected as stones of beauty, and "let in" in the sense of being displayed to view as a decorative addition to the temple. On the contrary, the temple builders were strictly utilitarian, and, laying these large slabs flat on the courses of masonry already raised, used them as binders, and built *on* them. The ends of figures sculptured in high relief can just be seen here and there on the slabs so utilized.

It is not improbable that these are the stones mentioned by Colonel Mackenzie as having been used by the then Rajah for the "repair of pagodas." I think, however, that Mr. Fergusson is in error in supposing that the Rajah used the materials of the Tope for "building the new town," in the sense of building any houses or paving any roads; for, though I searched carefully myself and made full inquiries, I could find no trace of any marbles in the town other than those just mentioned, and those I am now about to describe.

Two native gentlemen are now resident at Amarávati, direct descendants of the enterprising Rajah to whom Colonel Mackenzie refers. Their estate has for many years been in the hands of Government, being seized for arrears of revenue, and they live in a portion of the old palace buildings close to the temple, in receipt of a small pension from the State. These ex-zemindars, to whom I was much indebted for valuable assistance while at Amarávati, told me that some marbles from the Tope were kept inside the temple enclosure; and used their influence with the very intolerant Brahman priests there to such good purpose that the marbles were brought outside for my inspection. The stones will probably remain where I left them, and can be at any time removed to Bezwada or Madras. I give these here consecutive numbers 87, 88. But if the marbles are ever brought to England, and it is desired to identify these two by their numbers, it must be borne in mind that, not being at the stûpa itself, I did not put the numbers on them as I did with the others (though roughly), and they must be identified by description alone.

No. 87. (3 ft. 10 in. high and 3 ft. 7 in. broad, but broken into two fragments.) Portion of one of the smaller and less decorated dagobas of the Inner Enclosure. It may be compared with F., LXXVIII. 1. There are only a few figures on it. The base has the rail-ornament with the lotus-disc rail-bars, and pillars with lotus-disc ornaments beautifully carved.

Under the usual five steles is a five-headed cobra seated on a lotus. The guardian animals above the base are tigers. The band or frieze along the lower portion of the dome consists of the roll-ornament, another band higher up having a mixture of rails and animals.

No. 88. (2 ft. 3 in. by 1 ft. 1 in.) Base of one of the uprights which, according to Mr. Fergusson, divided the dagobas of the Inner Enclosure. It is broader than those yet found, but is something similar in design. The lowest portion is left rough. Above this is a band of lotus flowers and buds. And above this again a Buddha, seated under a chaitya-roofed canopy with nimbus round his head, and disciples attendant on him.

From the Śiva Temple on the river bank a fine broad street runs to the southern end of the town close to the Tope. On the western side of this street, under a tree where the village elders assemble for business purposes, and close to a site dedicated to *Mutiálamma*,[1] the village tutelary goddess, is another marble from the Tope. This may be called No. 89, though no numbers were painted on it.

No. 89. One of the Outer Rail coping-stones. The outside has the roll-ornament. The internal face is elaborately sculptured.

At the back is seen a walled enclosure, inside which is a male figure fully

[1] Every village in Southern India has its own particular goddess to whom prayers are offered. They are considered inferior deities, but specially honoured as protective powers. They have their little shrines and trees and images, and are the objects of adoration by the members of the village community.

draped lying at full length on a cot or slab of stone, apparently dead. In front of this are a number of trees and small houses with dome-shaped roofs. Into the picture from among the houses ride a party of five horsemen. Close to a house on the left, under which is a water-trough, are four people, one of them eagerly and earnestly addressing another who seems a young man. In the right foreground are some rocks, and close by these are two figures. One has lifted a cloth from the other who has seemingly been hiding under it, and the latter tries to run off.

Above the design is an inscription.

It ought not to be difficult to identify this scene, for the elements of which it is composed seem very distinctive in character, but at present I am unable to do so.

Before I leave the subject of the Amarávati marbles it will be desirable to notice, not only those now at Amarávati itself, but also those that I happen to know of at other places. These are as follows :—at Madras the tops of two pillars of the Outer Rail[1] and the casket, which I shall allude to presently; at Masulipatam a splendidly sculptured and excellently preserved dagoba, belonging to the Inner Enclosure, and a pillar of the Outer Rail; at Bezwada 22 marbles, presently to be described. My last discovery at Bezwada, in a deep water-course worn away under a hill side by unusual rains, consisted of two large statues of Buddha or Buddhist saints in the same marble that is used for the Amarávati sculptures. These may or may not have come from the Tope which is 17 miles away to the west. It is impossible to say.

Excluding these last as uncertain, we have by this list, as the state of discovery at present, 89 marbles at Amarávati, two at Madras, two at Masulipatam, and 22 at Bezwada. Total 115.

Mr. Fergusson (p. 182), speaking of the demolition of the Tope before Colonel Mackenzie's time, writes :—"All that the Rája discovered to reward his search was a "small relic casket which is now in the Madras Museum. It was apparently similar to "those found at Sanchi, but has no inscription and is of no intrinsic value;" and in a note he quotes a letter of Sir Walter Elliot's, describing the casket and stating that it had been sent to the Madras Museum. There I saw it in 1878. There is a circular stone case, with the top missing, and without inscription. Inside this is a small stone dagoba, and inside the dagoba is a vessel consisting of two equal hemispheres of thick crystal. This is empty.

Of the Masulipatam dagoba and pillar I am sorry to say I made no memorandum, and beyond the fact that they are richly carved and in excellent preservation, I can say but little. The dagoba is one of the larger ones, and may be compared with F., LXXVI.

Now for the marbles at Bezwada. These were separately numbered 9 to 30, being part of the collection of sculptures in the Library at that place.[2] If these marbles are all sent to Madras, or to England, it will not be difficult to distinguish them in spite of the numbers being concurrent, for the marbles found by me at Amarávati were roughly numbered in red paint, while those at Bezwada had their figures carefully painted in black by a skilled hand. I think it best to retain here the numbering which will be found on the marbles themselves, to avoid confusion, in spite of the apparent want of method so caused. When referring to the series at Amarávati those will be distinguished by the letter A, the Bezwada series by the letter B.

No. 9B. (2 ft. 10½ in. by 2 ft. 2 in.) Portion of a coping-stone having the roll-ornament. It apparently belongs to one of the older portions of the Outer Rail. The roll is supported by a *gaṇa*, and has a half-disc in its fold.

The back is cracked off. It is noticeable that the height of the actual roll-ornament is only 1 ft. 3 in., the more modern being 1 ft. 8 in. (compare F., Plate XCII. 5.)

---

[1] Measuring 2 ft. 6 in. in width. One has an inscription.

[2] Their position at the stûpa is unknown.

There is an inscription[1] above the frieze recording that the marble was presented by an elder of the church, but the name is wanting. The letters are of more antique character than any I have seen on other sculptures, which goes far to prove that this roll, of smaller size and with *gaṇas* for supporters, is older than that more commonly found.

No. 10B. Capital of a pillar, with a simple lotus-leaf ornament, probably part of one of the gateways. Circular. Diam. 1 ft. 8 in.

No 11B. A fragment (2 ft. 9. in. by 1 ft. 3 in.) similar in design to Nos. 26, 28B. Comparing these together it appears that they formed part of a projecting cornice. The inscription which this number bears lay underneath the projecting portion, and was thus protected from the effects of the weather. The back is not carved. The characters of the inscription are of much later date than those of No. 9B.

No. 12B. (Diam. 2 ft. 4 in.) Lotus-disc of the Outer Rail. The back is smoothed, polished, and round, like the Sánchi Rail-bars (*see my* No. 27A). The flanges have been cut off.

No. 13B. Another similar lotus-disc (diameter of lotus, 2 ft. 4 in.). The back has been smoothed in the same way, but the flanges have not been removed.

No. 14B. Lower portion of a pillar of the Outer Rail, internal face (height 3 ft. 3 in., breadth 2ft. 8 in.).

On a straight band of lotus-flowers and leaves stands a half lotus-disc, having, as usual, in the angles between it and the compartment above two half-opened lotus-buds.

Above is a figure-sculpture in three compartments. On the left is a prince and his wife seated on a couch with attendants about them. The prince's head having been broken off it is impossible to say whether the figure is intended to represent Prince *Siddhártha* or not. The central compartment shows the prince and his wife apparently receiving a guest whom he welcomes. Each of the principal persons is seated and attended by servants. The right compartment is too broken and weather-worn to be decipherable. All that can be seen is a figure, prostrate, and worshipping some one standing. The upper half is gone.

The back of the fragment has been cut or broken off, leaving only a portion visible of the mortice-hole which supported the flange of the disc.

No. 15B. Fragment (2 ft. 7 in. by 3 ft. 1 in.) of the coping stone of the Outer Rail, with sculpture on both sides.

This piece is in wonderful preservation. Every line of scroll-work on the roll is as clear and smooth as if it had just left the sculptor's hands. It has unfortunately been broken transversely, so that only a small portion remains of the sculpture on each side.

External Face.—The band above the main design is of lotuses; that below, of lotuses and animals. On the fold of the roll is an entablature representing the empty throne of Buddha, with the "wheel of the law" above, and two guardians with fans. Above this is a pillar supporting three *gaṇas* in attitudes of prayer and devotion.

Internal Face.—The sculpture is divided into four compartments. The left-hand upper division shows a seated figure. In the right upper division is a man bathing. He is seated cross-legged, and pours water over himself from a vessel which he holds over his head with both hands. Behind him stands a male atten-

---

[1] Note on this inscription by Dr. Burnell :—

"Read '*(ma)há theras(s)a mahádham(m)a kadhikas(s)a (? dánam).*'

"='*of the great thero, of the great preacher of the Law, (? the gift).*'

"On the omission of the reduplicated letters ⟨ s(s)a, m(m)a ⟩ see 'Palæography' (2nd edition), p. 30, also Goldschmidt's Reports.

"The only difficult word here is '*mahádhammakadhika*:' '*dhammakathika*' is used in Pali in the sense given above (see Childers' Dictionary *s.v.*), and this is the Prákrit equivalent of it. See Hemacandra (iv. 267), and Trivikrama (iii. 2, 4), by which the Sauraseni dialect puts, *optionally*, '*dha*' for '*tha*.' The example given (*kadhedi*) justifies this identification."

dant. The left-hand lower compartment has two figures apparently waiting on some one seated below. The marble is broken away, and the full design is not apparent. At the back of these figures is the rail design of pillars and discs, which may represent part of a building behind them, but it is impossible to say decidedly. The right compartment is also much broken away, and all that appears is a female head, three-quarter-face, with the hair elaborately braided and dressed. Behind the head are four symbols, detached, but I am unable to say what they are. I have a very poor photograph of this.

No. 16B. (7 ft. 0 in. by 2 ft. 8 in.) Another portion of the coping stone of the Outer Rail.

The external face shows the roll supported by three male figures, with hair braided and ornamented. On the left is the empty throne under a bo-tree with attendant worshippers. In the centre are two guardian figures bearing fans on either side of the "wheel of the law," while below is Buddha's throne and feet impressions. The emblem in the right-hand fold is a dagoba, surmounted by the tee, with clouds of umbrellas over it (as in "*Tree and Serpent Worship*," Plates XCI., XCIV., XCVII.).

On the internal face is an elaborate scene representing a castle with a procession of elephants issuing from the gate, while inside a feast is being held. The sculpture to the right shows the interior of the Palace with a group of twelve persons seated at table (a veritable table) in a balcony, beneath which a band of female dancers and musicians perform during the feast. The group of four dancers is admirably executed, the attitudes of the figures being very natural and graceful. It is noteworthy that the dancers are fully clothed from the waist downwards. To the right of the main group at the table is apparently an anteroom with attendants gossiping. The left half of the piece is occupied by the procession. A number of elephants are passing out of the gateway, each with a relic-casket or casket of offerings resting on its head. Each has its mahout and the usual trappings. The latter seem very similar to those in use in modern days. The animal in the foreground, for instance, carries the decorated head-cloth, the heavy body-cloth, and the swinging silver bell that warns foot-passengers of his approach.

No. 17B. (*a* and *b*). Two portions of the same pillar (*a*, 4 ft. 6 in. by 1 ft. 11 in.), (*b*, 3 ft. 4 in. by 1 ft. 11 in.). On one side is a *gaṇa* supporting a heavy vase with lotuses growing from it. In the midst of the flowers are two lions, while above is Buddha's throne with attendants. On the reverse the design is similar to the outer face of the pillars of the Outer Rail. It has one half lotus-disc and one whole one.

If this is one of the outer rail pillars, it is noticeable that its internal face is different to any of those yet discovered. Although the ruling idea is not unusual, I have found no pillar like it either amongst these marbles or those at Sánchi, Bharhut, or Buddha-Gaya, of which illustrations are published.

No. 18B. (Diameter of lotus, 2 ft. 8 in.) One of the discs of the Outer Rail. About one-third of the inner face has been broken off, but what remains constitutes a very beautiful and well-preserved specimen. The flanges are injured, but they have not been cut off.

One side, the outer, has the usual lotus-disc ornament.

On the internal face is a series of four designs in a circular band, occupying the space between the central boss and the external lotus-leaf rim. Above is a group of eight figures, men, engaged in carrying a large dish of offerings. All are in excited attitudes of devotion. The group occurs in many places in these sculptures, and may be found in three or four of the photographs and copies in Mr. Fergusson's work. Underneath this group to the right is one of a horse with saddle and bridle, unmounted, passing along treading on the heads and arms of *gaṇas* and surrounded by attendants with royal insignia.

The lower portion of the band is occupied by a bo-tree with attendant female worshippers.

On the left upper flange of the internal face of this slab is a portion of an inscription showing that the stone was the gift of two females, one of whom was named Báliká.

No. 19B. (3 ft. 5 in. by 2 ft. 8 in.) Lower portion of one of the pillars of the Outer Rail.

On one side, above a frieze of dolphins and lotuses, stands the usual half-disc. Above this is a design in three compartments. The central one has three fully-clothed male figures standing over the sacred feet of Buddha. On the left a similar figure armed with a bow stands in an attitude of adoration on the back of a dolphin. The right-hand compartment is broken away.

On the other side of the slab, on a similar half-disc and frieze, stands, in the central compartment, Buddha's throne with the feet-impressions, guarded by female attendants and shaded by a bo-tree, only the stem of which remains. The compartments on the right and left are much broken away, but each shows a portion of a male figure standing on a fish-monster.

From the similarity of the designs on each side it is impossible to say which was the inner and which the outer face of this pillar.

No. 20B. (Height 2 ft. 3 in., breadth 2 ft. 4 in.) Portion of a pillar similar to those of the outer rail, but having the mortice-holes cut square, showing either that the slab was not intended to support a disc, and therefore must have belonged to some other part of the stûpa, or that being originally one of the outer rail pillars it was subsequently made use of in another way. Only one face remains, the other apparently having been cut or split off. On this is one of the lotus-circles[1] having a fold of lotus-leaf above it. Above is a similar fold underlying the lotus-circle[1] above. The shaft between is cut into three compartments, but without figures. On the portion of the lower circle[1] that remains is a band of flowers and animals, two tigers and a bird being visible.

No. 21B. (Height 2 ft. 8 in., breadth 2 ft. 8 in.) A small fragment of the coping-stone of the Outer Rail. The external face has, in the fold of the roll, the empty throne standing between two worshippers and surmounted by the wheel of the law.

The internal face of the slab shows a prince, issuing from a gate of the Sánchi type which stands in front of a castle, accompanied by a procession of elephants, and surrounded by all the pomp of royalty. The sculpture is much weather-worn.

No. 22B. (Height 3 ft. 8 in., breadth 2 ft. 6 in.). Internal face of the base of a pillar of the Outer Rail.

On the usual half-disc are seen a number of people in adoration of Buddha's throne. Only a portion of this design remains, the upper half being broken away.

Only one side of this pillar was cut for the reception of the flange of the rail-disc, but it does not look like an angle pillar.

The back is broken or has been cut off.

No. 23B. (Diam. of disc, 2 ft. $9\frac{1}{2}$ in.) External face of one of the discs of the Outer Rail, the other face having been cut off, as well as the flanges. It has the usual lotus-circle.

No. 24B. (Height 3 ft. 4 in., breadth 2 ft. 4 in.) Central portion of a pillar of the Outer Rail, external face.

This has the complete lotus-circle, surrounded by a band of animals and flowers. Contrary to custom the boss of the circle has been sculptured. Usually the bosses are merely roughly indented with a few small circular dots, representing, probably,

---

[1] Or semi-circles. Portions only remain, and it does not appear whether this belongs to the upper or lower portion of the pillar.

the petals of the flower; but in this instance the boss bears a small winged lion of the Assyrian type.

The animal groups sculptured on the band surrounding the lotus are as follows:—

(1) a winged lion; (2) a bull charging; (3) two birds fighting; (4) a winged lion with a parrot's head; (5) *gaṇas* sporting with dolphins. (One stands behind a dolphin, and laughing, holds the animal's mouth open by means of a hook fixed in its upper jaw, while his companion exerts all his strength to pull something (the tongue?) out of its throat. The expression of face of the last *gaṇa*, irritated and apparently half-exhausted, is very well rendered.) (6) An animal, broken; (7) two birds; (8) a winged lion with a parrot's head; (9) a winged lion.

The back of this slab has been cut off, but the mortice-hole is visible.

No. 25B. (Height 1 ft. 10 in., breadth 1 ft. 1½ in.) A small fragment with a *gaṇa*, probably the base of a small pillar of one of the gateways.

No. 26B. (Length 2 ft. 1 in., breadth 1 ft. 3 in.) A portion of the same cornice as Nos. 11 and 28 (B) having a lotus-circle. On the side, in the same position as the inscription on No. 11, are the concluding letters of an inscription.

No. 27B. (2 ft. 11 in. high by 2 ft. 3 in. broad.) Portion of roll-ornament frieze, similar in style and width of the design to F., LVI. 2. Like that, it is a flat slab, thin, and cut off short above the upper band. This coincidence leads to a doubt as to whether both are, as Mr. Fergusson supposes, parts of the coping of the rail. Their appearance would lead to the supposition that they formed part of a frieze on the face of some wall, not the upper member of a rail.

No. 28B. (Length 3 ft. 3 in., breadth 1 ft. 3 in.) A fragment of the same portion of the *stūpa* as Nos. 11 and 26. It is a small piece of a cornice. It bears a lotus scroll, and at the end a vase with lotuses. It is this vase which proves that the fragment lay horizontally. Otherwise it might be taken for a fragment of a small pillar.

No. 29B. (1 ft. 6 in. by 1 ft. 2 in.) Portion of a small octagonal pillar. The shaft is decorated on three of its faces with a flower-and-bead ornament. Above the octagonal shaft the pillar is square, and on three of the sides are lotus half-discs. The back is broken off.

No. 30B. Fragment (about one-third) of one of the discs of the Outer Rail having the flange attached. On the flange was an inscription, but it is all gone with the exception of the tops of three letters.

The inside face represents the legend of King Sivi (*see* F., pp. 194, 224, 225). The king is seated in the centre holding the bird, which rests quietly on his left thigh. With his right hand he rejects the application of the two huntsmen who pray him for the delivery of their property. By the side of the king, on one of those high, basket-like, armless and backless seats common in these sculptures sits his minister. Behind are three female servants and three soldiers. Behind these again is a curious subject. A sort of screen is seen, or it may be a long, large basket. Above this appear four truncated heads of common people (hair cut short and not braided or dressed), perhaps belonging to decapitated prisoners. From the position of one it seems almost certain that the heads are without bodies; the others might possibly be standing behind a screen. Behind these again is a fringe of spear heads (a guard of soldiers, unseen because of the height of the basket?).

The huntsmen carry long wicker shields (used to the present day, stuck full of leaves and boughs to enable them to approach the birds). They have water-gourds slung over their shoulders. One carries a landing-net or snare, not unlike a modern butterfly-net.

Below is the scene where the monarch suffers a large piece of flesh to be cut off his left arm. The officer performs the operation with a broad-bladed knife. The back of this slab has been broken off.

---

§ G. CONCLUSION.

I HAVE now described as closely as lies in my power those marbles belonging to the Amarávati Tope of whose existence I am aware. Future excavations will result in the complete laying bare of all the remains of the monument, and it is much to be hoped that those excavations will be so carefully and scientifically conducted that nothing may be omitted which will hereafter give rise to vain regrets for the loss of opportunities for ever passed away. In such a case as this, the unearthing and removal of the disordered remains of the most beautiful Buddhist monument in all India, the difficulty lies in the fact that one faulty measurement or the wrong localization of a single stone may give rise to errors or difficulties that can never be remedied. Too great care and caution cannot be taken. Keenly sensible of my own omissions during that rather hurried week's work, I always hoped to return to the Tope, aided by Government with the services of a skilled surveyor and draughtsman, as well as a good photographer, so as to be able carefully to remedy all the defects of my own work, and then, with sufficient time at command, to proceed so cautiously with the excavation of the remainder that no difficulty might ever thereafter be felt in at once determining the size, shape, and position of any single stone now at the Tope, whether the marbles were removed to Madras or London or left where they lay. And now that I am led to believe that others are engaged, or will soon be engaged, in carrying out these excavations it is the more essential that I should point out prominently the defects of my own work, and give a list of the marbles which seem to me to require more careful examination and record than I was able to give them. These defects I had myself hoped to remedy. Perhaps those to whose lot it will fall to carry out the work will remedy them for me.

The centre of the circular hollow should be entirely excavated so as to leave bare the bottom and sides of the tank dug by the Rajah, which may possibly be found rich in marbles. Roughly speaking, this will consist of a square about the centre 33 ft. across, the rocky bottom of which will be found $24\frac{1}{4}$ ft. below the level of the platform, and a larger square outside this $102\frac{1}{4}$ ft. across, and $13\frac{1}{2}$ ft. below the platform level. All that is done must be done with Colonel Mackenzie's plan and section in hand. (F. XLVII.)

Amongst the notes and explanations left by Colonel Mackenzie, and published in the Asiatic Journal, vol. XV., 1823, p. 464, is one (p. 469) stating that a great many marbles were used to form a flight of steps to the "square tank of Shevagunga." Now Colonel Mackenzie's second, enlarged and as yet unpublished, plan, shows the "Shevagunga Tank" as lying on the east of the village. This was not brought to my knowledge while at Amarávati, and I was ignorant of its existence. It must be thoroughly examined, and the marbles, if possible, recovered.

It will be noticed that here and there my notes are deficient in the measurements of some of the marbles. This should be remedied.

Outside the platform the earth must be excavated to a depth of at least 2 ft. in order to uncover the zoöphorus frieze which Mr. Fergusson considers to have formed the base of the outside rail below platform level.

Especially at that lowest level, and more particularly at the four principal cardinal points where it is believed the entrance gates were, search should be made for coins, beads, and ornaments; for at the lowest level, *i.e.*, on the ground as it was in the earlier days of the building, the earlier coins may be expected to be found; and great care should be taken to record the place where each coin was found. For it will greatly assist the present investigation into the coinage and chronology of the Ândhrabhritya dynasty [1]

[1] Several coins of this dynasty having already been found here, it is reasonable to suppose that search will result in the discovery of others.

if it should be discovered that a certain class of coins is found at the lowest level, a certain other at a higher level after earth had begun to accumulate round the marble wall, and so on.

The inscription on the pillar (No. 17A.) in, as far as I can remember, about 12th or 13th century Telugu characters must be translated. A fac-simile taken off the stone itself lies at the Madras Museum.

The figure sculptures must be more carefully examined with reference to the introduction of *Nága* people. I omitted to do this, and my notes consequently lose very considerably in value.

Of individual stones I was anxious to examine more carefully Nos. 39, 40, and 42 (A.); to lift No. 25 (A.), and examine the marble No. 35 that lies underneath it; and to note the width of No. 37 (A.), and the distance between it and No. 28, so as to ascertain the size of the disc between them.

The inscriptions should be copied by estampages or rubbings according to the depth of the letters, several copies being taken at a time. They should be sent to the Madras Museum; to General Cunningham; and to Mr. James Burgess (Archæological Surveyor and Reporter to Government, Western India). Mr. Burgess has special facilities for translating inscriptions of all kinds in the Peninsular, and from being in constant communication with the best epigraphists of the day it is of paramount importance that he should be supplied with copies as soon as they are taken. Anything like colouring the letters on the stone itself to assist photography should be scrupulously avoided, as such a course may lead to error very difficult to remedy.

Finally, steps should be taken to recover more of the marbles used for the revetment of the well near the Tope; and it would be very desirable to open up negotiations with the Brahmans of the Śiva temple near the river for the recovery, if possible, of the marbles used in the walls of that building, replacing them with brick and plaster. Many of them are of large size, and possibly will be found to be covered with sculpture.

Before closing this paper there are a few points to which I am anxious to call attention connected with the neighbourhood of Amarávati.

In Colonel Mackenzie's plan of the town and river he mentions a certain "*Lingam Rock*" near the Śiva Temple. On the rocks near the temple in the river bed there are many inscriptions and carvings, but the characters are modern, and the carvings, with one exception, unimportant. The inscriptions simply commemorate the visits of pilgrims to the Śiva Temple, and I found none seemingly older than the 12th or 13th century. The principal one relates that in ŚŚ. 1245 (A.D. 1313) one Mallayya made a flight of steps, or ghaut, from the water's edge to the temple. I found none of greater importance than this. Of carvings there are several, well executed in the solid rock, mostly *lingams* and *Ganéśas*, appropriate to the worship of the temple.

While at Amarávati I examined the places marked "*Nackadeverdina*" and "*Cootch-tippa*" in Colonel Mackenzie's plan.

Both of these should be excavated. The first ("*Nakka-dévara-dinne*," or Jackal-god's mound") looks as if it had possibly been a small Tope dug up and destroyed. The centre is hollow, and it is surrounded by a circular mound higher than the ground level. The second ("*Kúrchi-tippa*," or chair mound") is more doubtful, but it deserves careful examination. Near this last are several of the ancient sepulchral stone-circles so common all along the banks of the Krishṇá.

About half a mile west of the fort of Dharaṇi-kòṭa is a rock in a field by the road side, having an important inscription which must be carefully examined. It is Colonel Mackenzie's "Shasanum Rock." The characters apparently belong to about the 11th century, judging from the copy I took of the first line. I had no time to pay to this inscription the attention it deserves. It is of considerable length, and commences (I think) "*Svasti, Sarvva lokáśraya Śrî Vishṇuvarddhaṇa.*"

INSCRIPTION STONE

PLATE IV.

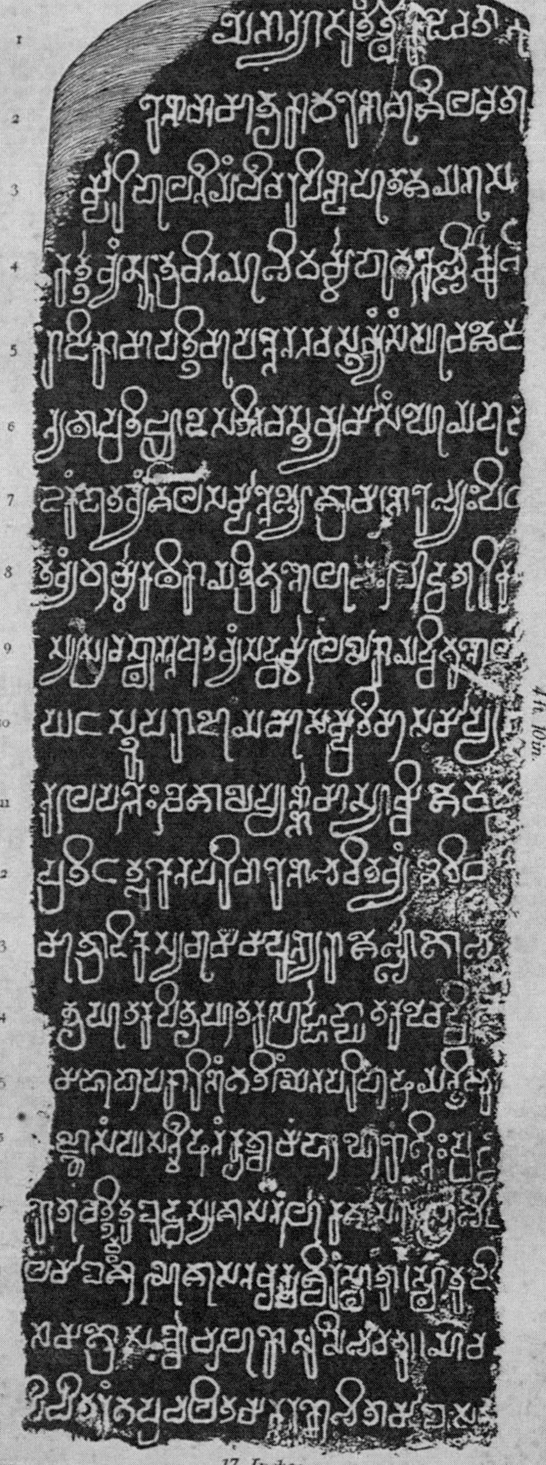

4 ft. 10in.

17 Inches

APPENDIX I.

NUMBERS 6 and 7 of Colonel Mackenzie's MS. drawings connected with the Amarávati Tope are copies of two inscribed stones. The larger one is called "Reduction from "an ancient Inscription on Stone found in Depaldinne at Amrawatty. The lower part "of the stone broken off." It is an inscription in 20 lines in a character apparently of about the 8th or 9th century A.D. The smaller (which is entered upside down) is called "Facsimile of an Inscription which was placed on the east side of the south gateway "of Depoldinna," and is dated August 1816. It is clear therefore that the former is the "*Inscription*" noted in Colonel Mackenzie's large plan (F., XLVII.) as having stood exactly at the north point of the circle.

With regard to the smaller of the two stones, Mr. Fergusson writes (p. 161, Appendix E., ix.):—"This is the most valuable of all the Amarávati inscriptions; but "unfortunately the slab has not come to England, and there is only a copy made by a "draughtsman to refer to. The title of Maharaja is distinct in the last line but one, "and the name following it appears to be *Yâdnya*, who was one of the last of the Andhra "kings." With due respect to General Cunningham (who has transliterated the inscription), I humbly submit that the copy is so exceedingly defective that his rendering of the doubtful "*Yâdnya Siri*" is, at the best, open to very reasonable question. But, however this may be, the stone has at present not been found, and it is useless to waste time in discussion. Possibly it might be found of invaluable aid to the chronology of the Tope, and it is earnestly to be desired that all possible search be made for it. Colonel Mackenzie distinctly states in the extract quoted above (p. 13) that the stone was sent to Calcutta, and I am not aware of any Amarávati marbles having been despatched from Bengal elsewhere. In Calcutta, therefore, this stone probably lies, and search may be rewarded by discovery.

It is with great pleasure that I announce the discovery of the larger inscription, an exact facsimile of which from the stone itself, forms Plate IV. attached to this Paper. This inscribed marble had disappeared since 1816. But, when examining the slabs which had lately been transferred from South Kensington to the British Museum and were lying in the temporary sheds on either side of the porch of the latter building, my eye happened to fall on a stone leaning against the wall and almost concealed by one of the sculptured marbles. I recognised at a glance the first few letters of the inscription as given by Prinsep in 1837, and further examination proved that at last this long-lost marble had been discovered. I was informed that it had found its way, not from the collection in South Kensington, but from the India Office Stores.

Colonel Mackenzie included it amongst some marbles entrusted to Major Cotgrave and sent down to Masulipatam (*see page* 13), but since then it had never been seen.

The inscription is of very great value palæographically, for the following reason:— In 1837, Mr. H. T. Prinsep, having received from Captain Cunningham a lithographed copy of the copy made by Colonel Mackenzie's clerk, published (in Vol. VI. of the Journal of the Asiatic Society of Bengal) a paper with facsimile, transliteration, and translation (p. 218), and *it is from this inscription that he tabulated his "Kistnah Alphabet."*

Now this so-called "Kistnah alphabet" has been accepted, on the strength of Prinsep's table, as a veritable and distinctively characteristic form of writing; and, so late as 1878, has been reproduced in Faulmann's "*Das Buch der Schrift*," (Vienna); but it will be seen at a glance that the peculiar square shape of the letters as given by Colonel Mackenzie's clerk is an exaggeration of the original, while Prinsep's table is an exaggeration of the clerk's; and that, so far from being a remarkable variety of the usual character, it is exactly of the type to be seen on the copper-plates of the period in other parts of India, only partaking of the upright form characteristic of the eastern as compared with the western inscriptions of the Peninsula.

The inscription in question may be very reasonably taken as the basis for an alphabet of the Lower (not the Upper) Krishṇá; but the alphabet can now be made out directly from the inscription itself, at last rendered available, and no longer from the clerk's copy.

Dr. Burnell's "Elements of South Indian Palæography," which contains four Eastern Chalukyan alphabets and four Veṅgi and Eastern Chalukyan inscriptions in facsimile, dated in the 4th, 7th, 10th, 11th, and 12th centuries, may be with great advantage consulted in reference to this question.

As readers will be interested to know what Prinsep wrote about this inscription, and as copies of the Journal in which his Paper appeared are not always available, I here reproduce a few extracts from his article :—

"In the Library of the Asiatic Society are ten manuscript volumes of drawings of sculpture, images, architecture, and inscriptions, forming part of the celebrated collection of the late Colonel MACKENZIE . . . . . As a specimen of the contents of these curious volumes, Captain Cunningham has kindly favoured me with the two lithographs numbered as Plates X. and XI. He has selected the two longest inscriptions from the volume No. 18, entitled 'Antiquities at *Amarávati*,' a town in the *Berar* province, situated on the *Kistna* River to the west of *Nágpur*."[1]

The inscription on Plate X. is the same given by Mr. Fergusson (p. 261, Appendix E., ix.) and referred to above. The other is the inscription now under discussion. Of this Prinsep writes :—

"The stone is noted down as 5 feet long by 17 inches in width. It is in very good preservation, as far as it goes, but the loss of the left half of its summit, and the fracture at the lowermost line, render it doubtful how much of the text may have preceded or followed that which remains."[2]

Then follows a discussion on the character and the means adopted for transliterating it.

"For the translation we are indebted to the Rev. Mr. YATES, whose critical knowledge of the Sanskrit enables him to give it the correct grammatical construction, which might evade an oral interpreter depending upon a vernacular explanation by the pandits."

Prinsep then gives the transcript, line by line, with comments on the engraver's inaccuracies, and continues :—

"The purport of the inscription refers, in all probability, to the foundation and endowment of some Buddhistic institution by the monarch of the day. His name cannot be extracted from the passages extant. It is evident, therefore, that history will gain nothing by the document; nor can any of the loose chronicles of the Hindu dynasties of *Telinga* or the *Carnatic* be expected to throw much light upon the period when *Amarávati* was subject to their hated opponents, the followers of the *Buddhist* creed."

It is, I think, unnecessary to reproduce Mr. Yates's "modified transcript," or his translation; for, believing that the inscription was complete as regards the length of the lines, he tried to make sense of the fragment by altering it at random, being guided merely by what he thought might have been dictated by a Pandit to an ignorant engraver who carved the letters more or less phonetically. Dr. Eggeling shows that we have only a portion of each line, and probably the smaller portion.

Professor Eggeling has been so kind as to furnish me with a transcription and translation of the fragment from a tracing of the lithograph published by Prinsep, which I made and sent to him; and these I now insert at length.

---

[1] This is a mistake.

[2] Both Mr. Yates and Mr. Prinsep thought that the inscription was complete as regarded the length of the lines.

TRANSLITERATION AND TRANSLATION BY DR. EGGELING (PROFESSOR OF SANSKRIT IN THE UNIVERSITY OF EDINBURGH).

1\. . . . . . ye nânyâsu[1] tîrtthika(?)-devatâsu . . .
2\. . . . . reṇa vâ mâtṛikâdhareṇa vâ śîlavatâ . . .
3\. . . . m[2] paripâlanîyaṃ chîvara-piṇḍapâta-śayanâsa . . .
4\. karttavyaṃ sûtravinayâbhidharmma[3]-pâṭhakair[4] bhbhikshu (bhiḥ ?) . .
5\. râjikâm âpattim âpannena na vastavyaṃ saṃghâvaśesha . . . .
6\. nyathâ pratichchhâde[5] sati na[6] vastavyam saṃgho yadâ . . . . .
7\. ṭekaṃ[7] dâtavyaṃ śilasampannebhyo śrâmaṇerebhyaḥ[8] piṭa (?) . . .
8\. tavyaṃ[9] dhârmmakathikâya[10] triguṇo lâbhaḥ bauddha-târika . . .
9\. sya avasthânan na dâtavyaṃ saddharmmalekhakâya dviguṇô l(âbhaḥ) . .
10\. ghaṭastûparâjâya[11] mâsam pratimâsam pû[12] . . .
11\. nulepanaiḥ vaiśâkha-pûrṇṇamâsyâm viśesha . . . .
12\. prati utsukena[13] parivâreṇa bhavitavyaṃ iti ma(?) . . .
13\. mâtrâdikasya vâ mama puṇyarâśêr bhbhâgô bha . .
14\. tṛighâtaka—pitṛighâtaka—arhhadghâtaka—devadvi(ja ?) . . .
15\. mahâpâpakâriṇâṃ gatiṃ[14] ye na paripâḷayanti[15] bhu[16] . . .
16\. jñâ saṃgha-sanmîḷanaṃ kṛitvâ mahâghoro(?)gniḥ pra . . .
17\. ro tâvat tishṭhatu[17] buddhasya śâsanaṃ lokaśâsanaṃ abhi[18] . .
18\. lamba[19]-sâkho[20] śâsanavṛikshaś chiraṃ sthâtu[21] ‖ sthâtu chi . . .
19\. samagro sarvvo cha loko sukhî bhavatu ‖ yâvad . . .
20\. —d vîchitaraṃga[22]-prachalita makarakshobhitâmbuś sa . . .

1\. . . (By whom) towards other deities of (Brahmanical) ascetics (?) . .
2\. . . or by one who holds the transcendental doctrine (*mâtrikâ=abhidharma*), or by one of good character . . .
3\. should be kept up the mendicant's garment and almsgiving and sleeping . .
4\. should be done by those who study the *Sûtra*, *Vinaya*, and *Abhidharma* (the three divisions of the Buddhist canon), (by ?) mendicant friars . . .
5\. —?—by (or with ?) one who has fallen into misfortune should not be dwelt. A transgression that can be remitted by the assembly . . .
6\. if there is otherwise shelter, one should not dwell. When the assembly . .

NOTES BY R. S. ON DR. EGGELING'S TRANSCRIPTION.

1 Prinsep, in his table, makes this character a short initial *ă*, but where it occurs in line 19 he renders it *su*. And to the character which really represents *ă* in line 9 he gives the value *sú*. (*See* his Table of Alphabets and the characters respectively for *ă*, *su*, *sú*, in lines 1, 4, 9, 14, 17, 19 of this inscription.)
2 This form of final *m* with *virâma* is common in this inscription. (*See* lines 6, 18, 20.)
3 The doubling of a letter preceded by *r* is very common in inscriptions of this period.
4 *ṭha*. The letter is injured, but the reading is almost certainly correct.
5 The form *chchh* is noticeable.
6 The clerk's copy omits the characteristic side stroke of the *na*.
7 Dr. Eggeling doubtfully reads this *ṭe*.
8 *–maṇe—*. The form of *ṇe* is unusual.
9 *–vyaṃ*. The *anuswâra* is omitted in the clerk's copy.
10 *dhâ* erroneously engraved for *dha*.
11 The clerk's copy reads *ghaṭa saparâjâya* through a careless omission.
12 *pû*. This form is repeated in line 11, *pûrṇṇa*, but the shape is peculiar.
13 Prinsep read the letters *utsu* as *ṭatra ;* and follows this in his Alphabet.
14 The *anuswâra* is rather awkwardly placed for want of space over the *ti*.
15 *–ḷa—*. This form is apparently unique. The Sanskrit has no such letter, the use of which is confined to the Dravidian languages. Prinsep rendered it *ḍha*, both here and in line 16, where it occurs again.
16 This letter is very badly given in the clerk's copy. Prinsep leaves it alone.
17 The *shṭha* has been carelessly omitted by the engraver, and subsequently entered below very clumsily.
18 The form taken for *a* may possibly be *â*. But it is much injured. The lower curve seems a little different from the *a* in line 14.
19 (*See note* 2.)
20 The interpolated compound rendered *shṭha* by Dr. Eggeling (*see note* 17) is immediately over the syllable *śâ*.
21 The clerk joins by mistake the top of the *t* and the first stroke of the double line dividing the verses.
22 Another error of the copyist gives this letter the form of *śa*.

7. —?—it is to be given, to respectable novices . . .
8. —?—for one who promulgates the Law there is a threefold benefit—redeeming (?) the Buddhist . . .
9. shelter is not to be given; for the copier of the good Law there is a twofold benefit . .
10. ? to the royal (*ghaṭ*—?) tope,—month—month by month . . .
11. with unguents on the full moon of the month Vaiśâkh, special (or speciality) . . .
12. ?—(by) a zealous retinue —there is to be," thus . . .
13. (may there be) a share of the heap of merit for me, and before me, for my (father and) mother[1] . .
14. (mo)ther-killing—father-killing—Arhat-killing—Gods-twice-(born)[2]— . . .
15. of those who commit great sins, who do not mind their future state (?)
16. A most terrible fire having caused the closing[3] of the Assembly . . . .
17. —?—? So long may stand Buddha's law as the Law of the world !—
18. the hanging-boughed tree of the Law, may long stand ! May long stand . .
19. may the whole and entire world be happy ! As long as . . .
20. (As long as the ocean ?) has its waters agitated by sea-monsters roused by the tossing of the waves !

Dr. Eggeling writes :—

" You will see from the enclosed transliteration and partial rendering that the document supplies no historical data, and that it is indeed impossible to get from it any connected sense of the Buddhist rules of conduct or the conditions under which certain benefits are apparently held out to devout Buddhists by the grantor; since only the first (and perhaps smaller) portion of each line has been preserved."

Professor Eggeling thinks that the inscription belongs to the sixth century at latest, and compares the character with that of the Chera inscriptions, " for instance, that of the " Mercara plates (A.D. 467), though it is true that writing did not greatly change during " the fifth to eighth centuries." The question is one of considerable interest; for, since we know that the Brahmanical Chalukyas conquered the Vengi kingdom early in the seventh century (A.D. 605 ?), if this inscription is of later date than that of their conquest it will be sufficient proof that Buddhism was not finally stamped out by them, and that they were tolerant of religious systems differing from their own. I have expressed my opinion above that the inscription belongs to about the eighth century, and I am content to leave the decision in the hands of those more skilled than myself in South-Indian Palæography.

---

1 Dr. Eggeling remarks that it is a common thing to find in Buddhist grants that some blessing is invoked to the grantor's parents and relatives; and he mentions several instances from the Kudâ inscriptions supplied to him by Mr. James Burgess in his forthcoming Part (the tenth) of the Archæological Survey of Western India, where formulæ very similar to the one above are used.

2 Brahmans?

3 *sanmî*—for *sammî*—.

APPENDIX II.

AFTER this paper was in type I sent a set of proofs to Sir Walter Elliot, whose excavations at the Amarávati Tope have been so often referred to by Mr. Fergusson and other writers, and he has done me the kindness to put on paper some notes of his labours in the form of a letter. This I do not propose to print *in extenso*, as it was not written for publication; but, with his permission, I proceed to give all that it contains of value or interest. He writes as follows:—

"My excavations were made in 1845. I was very hard worked, being on a special commission to investigate abuses, and my mission only lasted a few months."

The date (1840) given above (p. 20) as that of these excavations is, then, erroneous. It was taken from Mr. Fergusson's work, and from the statements of Dr. Balfour and Mr. Taylor (pp. 20, 21).

"I only knew of the existence of Dîpâldinne from Colonel Mackenzie's Paper in the "Asiatic Researches." When I visited the spot I simply saw a rounded mound or hillock, with a hollow or depression at the summit, but without a vestige or indication of an architectural structure, or even a fragment of wrought stone, to show that a building had once stood there, *every fragment of former excavations having been carried away and burnt into lime.*"

The italics are mine. This statement is very important, and serves both to throw light on the past, and to act as a warning for the future. We learn from it that the marbles seen by Colonel Mackenzie had vanished from Amarávati. I believe there is no record of any more than 11 having ever been sent by him from Amarávati, though it is possible that the "33 large slabs" seen by Dr. Benza in the market-place of Robertson Pettah, the newly created suburb of Masulipatam (p. 20), may have formed part of them. Colonel Mackenzie records the positions of 132 slabs. As Sir Walter Elliot found the ground blank, and obtained his slabs by excavating a part of the mound to the south-east, which was untouched by Mackenzie, it must, I think, be concluded that these 132 slabs had been removed. We know of 11 having been sent by Colonel Mackenzie to Masulipatam, seven of which went to Calcutta, and the other four probably to England. One of these last, the larger inscription stone, which forms the subject of Appendix I., was found in the India Office stores, and it is reasonable to conclude that the other three kept it company. This leaves 121 to be accounted for. Dr. Benza gives us the possible clue to 33. Now, since Sir Walter Elliot saw only four or five of these at Masulipatam in 1851, we must conclude that the remainder either found their way to Madras or disappeared into the possession of natives who knew not their value. Granted that these 33 were all of Mackenzie's excavation, and that the 18 of Mackenzie's now in England (p. 30) were all different to these (which does not at all necessarily follow) we have 51 marbles accounted for out of the 121 we are searching after. Balance, 70. I believe that there is in no writing yet made public any reference to these marbles, or any trace of their having been removed from Amarávati, and it must therefore be assumed that they have disappeared. Sir Walter Elliot, no doubt, has solid foundation for his statement that every fragment that remained had been carried away and burnt into lime. This was the information he received at Amarávati, and the exasperating conclusion to which we are inevitably drawn is that these 70 sculptures remained on the spot and were ruthlessly destroyed by the villagers between the years 1817 and 1845.

This will almost certainly be the fate of all marbles left at Amarávati without competent guard.

Sir Walter Elliot goes on:—

"I began to dig quite haphazard, I think about the S.W. (?) side of the mound, and the first object that rewarded my search was one of the lions lying prostrate that had surmounted the side of the entrance. I then uncovered some of the stones of the Rail standing upright but not continuously, and penetrated into an apparent restoration of a part of the entrance, as if for the construction of a small temple out of the ruins of the main building. I made a rough sketch of this on the spot . . . . I also tried on returning to Madras to make a restored elevation of the *sthupa* from the measurements, but the result brought out a broad depressed instead of a narrow compressed cone, as represented in the sculptures . . . This sketch . . . . . was saved out of the wreck of my papers in a half-rotted state. I had not the slightest idea at first what was the character of the structure, which dawned on me slowly as the excavations proceeded, and I saw that the pieces found corresponded with the form repeated so frequently on the sculptured representations of a dehgope."

Sir Walter gives me two slight representations of his "broad depressed" cone and "narrow compressed" one. By the former he means a tumulus of shape similar to that at Sánchi; by the latter, a dagoba such as those seen in the sculptures, with a diameter at the base small as compared with the height of the dome.

"I believe that all the pieces now in the Museum, with the exception perhaps of the piece that had found its way to the Museum previously, were the fruits of my search. Those to which you refer as noticed by Benza have a different history. There were a few stones, the remains, I believe, of Mackenzie's examination (?) which were brought down after Sir Fredk. Adam's visit to Bunder for the embellishment of Robertson Pettah. I inquired for these during my stay of several weeks at Bunder in 1851 (in 1845 I never crossed the Kistna, continuing the whole time in Guntoor) and found no trace of them. But I learnt that Mr. Alexander, the Master Attendant, who had a taste for picking up curiosities, had appropriated them, and they were in his compound, where I saw them. I think four or five in number. He said he had removed them with Mr. Porter's permission to save *the best of them from the injuries they were receiving in the Bazaar*, and the others . . . . had disappeared.

"On my arrival at Madras, in Council in 1854, I caused a claim to be made for the pieces in Mr. Alexander's garden through Mr. Goldingham, who succeeded me as Commissioner; but I had come down in bad health, suffering from fever, and was obliged to go home for six months. I therefore do not know the result of my motion, but I suppose Goldingham got them and sent them down."

I have found eighteen of Colonel Mackenzie's marbles amongst those in England, and Sir Walter Elliot would seem to be mistaken in his conclusion that the only marbles in England are those excavated by him. The only marbles to be seen at Masulipatam in 1851 were those in Mr. Alexander's compound, four or five in number, though in 1837 there were 33 in the market-place. We have no record of such a fact, but it is possible that the remainder had been sent to Madras previous to 1851. If not, then the eighteen in England must be different ones altogether, and it would be interesting to learn how they got there. The passage in italics (my own) is again noteworthy.[1]

With regard to the four or five stones appropriated by Mr. Alexander, I may mention that when I left Bunder last, in April 1879, they were still in his compound. Two fragments were lying under a tree with some small traces of sculpture visible but almost entirely destroyed. Two others, in very fine preservation, stood erect ornamenting the drive up to the house door. I have alluded to these above (p. 30). The two lying down were small fragments and do not appear to have been of importance. The history of Mr. Alexander's connection with the marbles is interesting. He appears to have resolutely maintained that they were his own property, and he so persistently refused to hand them over that Government finally passed an order, denying his right but presenting them to him as an act of grace. There they remained till, in 1877 or 1878, Government purchased them from Mr. Alexander's executors. They were ordered to be removed to Madras, but this had not been done previous to my leaving the district.

---

[1] In a subsequent letter Sir Walter Elliot tells me that he was, in 1851, so hard-worked that he did not visit the market-place, and cannot tell whether there were any marbles there or not. Possibly there were. If so, the marbles afterwards sent down to Madras were probably the same. Sir Walter says that he was instrumental in having them sent. They were probably sent by Mr. Goldingham in 1855 or 1856, as stated on pp. 20, 21.

Sir Walter Elliot states :—

"There was a miniature representation of a dehgope in sandstone, which had formed the summit of one of the single pillars, one of which stood on each side of the entrance within the *paridakshina*. This lay for some time in the entrance of my house at Madras. I told the curator of the Central Museum to send for it when I left that residence . . . but whether it was so taken I do not remember.

(I have not observed this at the Madras Museum, and it would be interesting to know if it is there or not.)

"I also made application for the vase or casket found by Vasa Reddi when he ruined the tope to make a tank, which I had discovered when at Guntoor had been sequestrated with the rest of the Zemindar's property and was lodged in the Guntoor Court. This I got through the interposition of the Sudr, and placed it in the Central Museum."

As I have stated, this casket is now in the Madras Museum.

In a subsequent letter Sir Walter Elliot tells me that he always believed and maintained that the marble rail "surrounded a *sthupa* of vast size which arose immediately within it, "having only an open corridor or pathway round it; the rail richly sculptured inside and out and the "opposite wall of the *sthupa* also enriched with carving."